GAYLORD S

Sartre's
Ethics
of
Authenticity

Sartre's
Ethics
of
Authenticity

Linda A. Bell

The University of Alabama Press
Tuscaloosa and London

Library of Congress Cataloging-in-Publication Data

Bell, Linda A.
Sartre's ethics of authenticity.

Bibliography: p.
Includes index.
1. Sartre, Jean Paul, 1905–   —Contributions in
ethics. 2. Ethics, Modern—20th century. I. Title.
B2430.S34B35 1989   171'.2   86-19284
ISBN 0-8173-0335-9

British Library Cataloguing-in-Publication Data available

Contents

Acknowledgments

Permission to quote excerpts from works of Jean-Paul Sartre is acknowledged gratefully as follows:

Anti-Semite and Jew, by Jean-Paul Sartre, translated by George J. Becker, © 1948 by Schocken Books, Inc. Used by permission of Editions Gallimard and Schocken Books.

Being and Nothingness, by Jean-Paul Sartre, translated by Hazel E. Barnes, © 1956 by Philosophical Library. Used by permission of Editions Gallimard, Methuen & Co., and Philosophical Library.

Cahiers pour une morale, by Jean-Paul Sartre, © 1983 by Editions Gallimard. A complete translation of *Cahiers pour une morale* is forthcoming from The University of Chicago Press. Permission to translate and publish excerpts was granted by Editions Gallimard and The University of Chicago Press.

Critique of Dialectical Reason, by Jean-Paul Sartre, translated by Alan Sheridan-Smith, © 1976 by VERSO (New Left Books). Used by permission of Editions Gallimard and VERSO (New Left Books).

ACKNOWLEDGMENTS

The Devil and the Good Lord, by Jean-Paul Sartre, translated by Kitty Black and Sylvia George Lesson, © 1960 by Alfred A. Knopf, Inc. Used by permission of Editions Gallimard and Alfred A. Knopf, Inc.

Saint Genet, by Jean-Paul Sartre, translated by Bernard Frechtman, © 1963 by George Braziller, Inc. Used by permission of Editions Gallimard and George Braziller, Inc.

What Is Literature? by Jean-Paul Sartre, translated by Bernard Frechtman, © 1965 by Methuen & Co. Used by permission of Editions Gallimard, Methuen & Co., and Harvard University Press. In 1988 Harvard University Press reissued this work in a volume called *What Is Literature and Other Essays*.

Preface

Is a coherent, viable Sartrean ethics possible? This question has guided much of my work and pondering since I encountered Sartre's writings in graduate school many years ago. Since that time, Sartre has died, and his popularity, even in philosophical circles, has waned.

Many philosophers believe—indeed, the prevailing opinion seems to be—that Sartre's published work renders ethics impossible, not just problematic, that Sartre's death ended any chance of his "correcting" his earlier views and developing a consistent ethics. Critic after critic has asserted that Sartre's early views of consciousness and freedom are themselves sufficient to undermine any attempt to develop an ethics thereon. Many have commented on the "radical conversion" Sartre's own thought underwent between his earlier existential writings and his later, more Marxist work, the latter supposedly more promising for ethics. Yet the reiterated claims and arguments are not convincing, for reasons that are developed in the following pages.

Year after year I have returned to Sartre's writing, analyses, and arguments which have special bearing on ethics, seeking alternative interpretations of some of the more problematical passages. I have tried to juxtapose writings not usually connected with each other, sometimes treating brief remarks, asides, and repeated but infrequently used concepts as aids in solving the mystery of Sartre's broader meaning.

In the course of all this, I have worked out answers to some common questions and some not-so-common questions about Sartrean ethics. I find these answers satisfying; they seem to be based on an adequate interpretation of what Sartre says. Familiarity may have made me overly comfortable with my interpretation, however, just as I have long thought the familiarity of the prevailing interpretation of Sartre has led numerous critics to ignore much of what he says and thus fail to probe other possible meanings beneath the superficial ones. I can only hope that some will read my answers and their supporting arguments with enough care and sympathy to uncover problems and perplexities therein and thereby carry forward a deeper probing of the possibilities of Sartrean ethics.

Many have already contributed enormously to my understanding of Sartre, although no doubt relatively few of them would clearly recognize their contributions. Calvin O. Schrag introduced me as a graduate student to Sartre's work and later gave me an opportunity to continue work on Sartre at a National Endowment for the Humanities Summer Seminar. At that seminar, I met William L. McBride, a colleague of Schrag's, who generously gave his own time to any in the seminar who sought his advice or assistance. His critiques of my work have been invaluable in many ways.

Others have read and critiqued sections of this manuscript at various stages in its development. Dieter Turck, my dissertation director, responded perceptively and with great care to draft after draft of my

dissertation on Sartrean authenticity and moral judgment and helped me complete a Ph.D. in a department
which at that time was not particularly enthusiastic
about any aspect of Sartre's philosophy. John Beversluis, Susan Fox Beversluis, C. G. Luckhardt, Joseph
S. Catalano, Hubert L. Dreyfus, Thomas R. Flynn,
Nancy Fraser, and Robert V. Stone have all guided me
toward clearer formulations of my ideas and arguments and away from some serious errors.

Toward the end of this process, several who made
notable contributions vis-à-vis the entire manuscript
deserve special recognition. Albert C. Skaggs was invaluable as a stylist and proofreader. Especially valuable were creative suggestions for gender-neutralizing
much of my writing. R. Barton Palmer checked and
corrected my translations of material from the re-
cently published *Cahiers pour une morale.* Finally, the
two reviewers for The University of Alabama Press
(whose identity is unknown to me) were enormously
helpful, as was Roy Grisham, who edited the manuscript.

Others have contributed to the manuscript more
materially. Several typists typed and retyped various
sections; Martha Jordan and Lynn Farnham were particularly helpful at the last, as I put all the sections
together. Other support included released time granted
by the dean of the College of Arts and Sciences at
Georgia State University, a tremendously important
support in a situation where the teaching load is high.

Finally, the reader needs to be acknowledged by anyone who claims to have learned anything from Sartre.
As Sartre says in *What Is Literature?,* without the
reader, "the book falls back and collapses; there remain
only ink spots on musty paper." *With* a reader there is
the possibility of collaboration—between the author
and the reader—to produce the book. Because this

book is an investigation of the possibilities of Sartrean ethics, my appeal to the reader's freedom goes beyond the appeal to collaborate in the production of this book; rather, it invites the reader to continue and improve on what I have done, just as I have tried to continue and improve on the work of other sympathetic critics of Sartre.

LINDA A. BELL

Sartre's
Ethics
of
Authenticity

1

Is an Ethics of
Deliverance and
Salvation Possible?

> These considerations do not exclude
> the possibility of an ethics of
> deliverance and salvation.
> —Sartre, *Being and Nothingness*

In one of his best-known works, Jean-Paul Sartre observes that play, "which has freedom for its foundation and its goal, deserves a special study which . . . belongs rather to an *Ethics*."[1] Like other remarks Sartre promised to explain someday in a book on ethics (a promise unkept), this statement haunts anyone who reads *Being and Nothingness*, especially the reader interested in ethics. Similarly, Sartre's readers are tantalized by his footnote references to authenticity, "a self-recovery of being which was previously corrupted," and to "an ethics of deliverance and salvation."[2] Many readers, however, have concluded that authenticity and such an ethics of deliverance and salvation are impossible if, as Sartre says, "man is a useless passion" and "it amounts to the same thing whether one get drunk alone or is a leader of nations."[3] Still others, undeterred by the latter claims, have no doubt reacted with hopeless dismay when Jean Genet is depicted as a "saint" and when the most heroic characters in Sartre's plays, novels, and short stories are presented not only with "dirty hands" but also as playing, even consciously, a "game" of "loser wins."

For Sartre's friends and foes alike, problems of ethics remain unresolved. In his early work Sartre denied the existence of God and, claiming that without God everything is permitted, still pronounced an adverse moral judgment on any who would deny their own freedom or that of others. With no God to create them, Sarte proposed, human beings have no "nature" or essence apart from that which *they* create; even so, he argued, given an awareness of freedom as the foundation of all values, an individual cannot but will his or her own freedom and, along with this freedom, that of others. How, critics have asked time after time, can Sartre make moral judgments after denying the existence of both God and objective moral values? How can he maintain that individuals create their own essence yet condemn those who choose to see themselves or others as determined or enslaved? Even if freedom is the foundation of all values, why should one *will* freedom? Consistency may seem to demand this, but must one be consistent? If there are no objective values, how can Sartre condemn, except idiosyncratically, anyone who chooses to value inconsistency—as do those in bad faith?

For Sartre, those who will their own freedom and that of others are *authentic*; yet he seems to have little to say about such individuals as he develops his views of freedom, bad faith, and relations with others. In fact, from their reading of *Being and Nothingness*, many students of Sartre have concluded that all human beings are in bad faith; thus inauthenticity is viewed as inevitable and relations with others as hopelessly premised on denial of freedom. When Sartre elsewhere presents characters or individuals who seem to affirm their own and others' freedom, he depicts them as alienated, as mired in ambiguity, as having "dirty hands," or as playing a game of "loser wins." Are we to conclude that the authentic are no less alienated than those in bad faith? Does the ambiguity of the human condition permeate even the attempt to will one's own freedom and that of others, thereby making inevitable bad faith? Is the recognition of dirty hands and of the game of loser wins related to authenticity? If so, how?

Sartre affirms that each person must choose her or his own values. He makes it clear that nothing warrants or justifies making one choice over another. He decries the "seriousness" of those who take values as given and their existence and behavior as justified through such values. Yet even such a sympathetic critic as Thomas C. Anderson objects that Sartre's and Simone de Beauvoir's "willingness to put their lives and honor on the line in support of human dignity seems to bear witness to the very spirit of seriousness they so scornfully reject."[4] It is possible to create values without slipping, on the one hand, into the indecisiveness and tolerance of everything so often ascribed to ethical relativists, or, on the other, into the seriousness that Sartre explicitly rejected?

In his early philosophical writings, Sartre emphasized freedom, claiming that human beings are free even to the extent of choosing their own chains. It is a manifestation of this freedom that we choose, for example, whether something like a withered arm will be a handicap or when the pain inflicted by a torturer becomes too great to bear.

Some, such as Herbert Marcuse, in an article on Sartre's existentalism, written in 1948, have understood such claims about freedom to mean that freedom is absolute and unalterable and, consequently, offers "a most handy justification for the prosecutors and executioners in whose hands . . . this freedom has shrunk to a point where it is wholly irrelevant and thus cancels itself."[5] These critics reject as "idealistic mystifications" and "mere ideology" Sartre's early claims about freedom and the existentialist position in which the claims are embedded. The critics generally see, as did Marcuse in a postscript to his article, Sartre's later writings on scarcity and revolution as indications of his own "radical conversion."[6] Yet in an essay, "Materialism and Revolution," published in *Les Temps Modernes* in 1946, Sartre himself rejects, as Marcuse acknowledges, such "inner freedom that man could retain in any situation" as "a pure idealistic hoax," reducing freedom to "the autonomy of thought" after "[separating] thought from action."[7]

Are these critics correct in maintaining that Sartrean authenticity—based, so they allege, on bourgeois freedom—can support only an individualistic ethics reflecting the values of the status quo? Did Sartre thus reject his earlier claims about authenticity as he moved on to discuss revolution and its importance? Or is Sartre himself a better judge of his own development when he claims that there has been an "evolution" in his thinking but not a "break"?[8]

Finally, Sartre generally presents relationships of human beings with one another in a rather dismal light. In *Being and Nothingness* he suggests that our relationships with others—including love—are premised on an impossible demand: that we capture their freedom. Many have seen in this, and in other writings, confirmation that Sartre is committed to an individualism that precludes authentic relationships with others. Such critics have ignored not only interviews in which Sartre speaks in glowing terms of his relationship with de Beauvoir but also various other accounts of human relationships which do not fit the patterns laid out in *Being and Nothingness*. Can all of these claims about human relationships be squared, or are critics right in saying that Sartre's early position commits him to an individualism at odds with his more mature view?

On the basis of Sartre's writings, I develop answers to these questions and conclude that there is implicit in these writings a coherent and viable ethical position. In my interpretation of Sartre's various statements I frequently relate Sartre's points to similar or contrasting moves made by ethicists familiar to British and U.S. students of philosophy. Parallel or relevant arguments, claims, and challenges from David Hume, Immanuel Kant, G. W. F. Hegel, Karl Marx, R. M. Hare, W. T. Stace, and others not only serve to illuminate what Sartre is doing but should assist the continuing dialogue between opposing traditions in philosophy.

These questions can be divided into five sets of questions. The first set focuses on whether Sartre can consistently condemn anything, except idiosyncratically, except, that is, as a reflection of his particular choice of values. Specifically, can Sartre consistently affirm that human beings are free and responsible creators of value and meaning, as well as condemn bad faith? And does this condemnation hold for the rest of us, regardless of our freely chosen values?

The second set of questions bears on individual alienation. For Sartre, a human being is an ambiguous being, a tension between opposites. Such beings can never quite become what they are, nor can they ever wholly divorce themselves from what they are not. Unable to coincide with themselves, they similarly are unable to coincide with their values. An individual's values are never completed or perfected; whatever they may be, they are set at a distance by the individual's freedom to reaffirm those values or to choose new ones. Thus "human reality is by nature an unhappy consciousness with no possibility of surpassing its unhappy state."[9] Alienation appears inevitable, given what it is to be a human being. Does this mean—as some have thought—that bad faith similarly is inevitable? Can the alienation of bad faith be avoided or overcome? Would the alienation of authenticity differ from the alienation of bad faith? How?

The third set of questions issue from Sartre's voluntarism with respect to values, his affirmation that each person must choose her or his own values. Many have claimed either that such relativism vis-à-vis values renders action impossible or that it leads to logical absurdities. Sartre's recognition of the ultimate futility of action complicates matters by adding a psychological demoralization. If all actions are futile, and in this respect equivalent, is not the persistence of the authentic individual pointless? Can a morality demand the impossible?

In the fourth set of questions, the central question is: What about societies? In the *Critique of Dialectical Reason*, Sartre developed what he then regarded as a form of Marxism but later viewed as only "close to Marxism."[10] He condemned certain social structures and approved revolutions of the alienated and oppressed against alienating and oppressive institutions. Is alienation thereby overcome? It seems that it is not. Rather, alienation—now in the forms of scarcity and of the opposition between the group and the ineradicable freedom and individuality of its members—continues to threaten, eventually bringing down the new institutions, even if they are less oppressive than their predecessors. Cannot there be some progress, however? Do some new institutions merit our praise and support even if they do not completely overcome alienation?

In the fifth set of questions, the focus is on more intimate human relationships. Much Sartre scholarship has foundered on what seems an insurmountable problem with these relationships. Sartre's best-known works contain extraordinarily bleak views of love and intimacy, typified by the famous line from *No Exit*, "Hell is—other people!"[11] Those familiar with *Being and Nothingness* are likely to accept Iris Murdoch's characterization of its account of love as a "battle between two hypnotists in a closed room."[12] If Sartre's analyses of love, desire, masochism, and sadism in *Being and Nothingness* indicate the full range of interpersonal relationships, then the authentic individual may seem doomed to solitude and sequestration from others even though that individual may join forces with others on a social level. Should these analyses, however, be taken as exhaustive of such relationships? What should we make of Sartre's later claim that "[beginning] with Saint Genet I changed my position a bit, and now I see more positivity in love"?[13]

These questions presented above become especially significant when placed alongside Sartre's answers in the context of traditional ethics. As an example, consider the first question, regarding the possibility of consistently judging bad faith to be morally wrong. Sartre assumes (1) when one chooses (e.g., freedom), one chooses for all people; and (2) in so doing, one thereby makes a "moral judgment" condemning those who recognize freedom but who try to avoid choosing either their own freedom or that of others. In making these claims, Sartre seems to move either toward a Kantian ethics that bases morality on universalizability or toward an ethics that bases all morality on telling the truth and all immorality on the lie. Given Sartre's views of the diminished role of reason in the creation of value, the former move is not open to him. Similarly, the latter move is problematic for a voluntarist such as Sartre. Any attempt to base all immorality on the lie leaves unanswered—and unanswerable—the question, Why is lying wrong? In

21

arguing against a contemporary eighteenth-century moralist, David Hume recognized this difficulty; and the question remains as problematic for any who try to interpret Sartre this way as it was for Hume's antagonist. In Chapter 3 of the present work, these two alternative interpretations of Sartre's "moral judgment" (and of his claim that one chooses for everyone) will be challenged and a third interpretation proposed—namely, that what is involved in Sartre's moral judgment is purely analytic, given what it means to choose moral values and to adopt the moral point of view.

Chapter 4 deals with the second set of questions, those concerning the relation of alienation to bad faith. In that chapter two kinds of alienation will be distinguished. One kind of alienation is inevitable: one can never coincide with one's goals, with onself, or with others. Attempts to overcome such alienation are futile; often they are seen as involving circles and self-enclosures (as the futility itself is sought). These attempts involve the other kind of alienation—the alienation imposed on oneself in bad faith—which is avoidable and can be overcome. It is with respect to the latter, not the former, that Sartre can be seen as subscribing to a dialectic much like Hegel's famous master/slave dialectic. Distinguishing these two types of alienation from one another will enable us to see why Sartre both affirms a dialectic when discussing the life of Jean Genet, yet denies a dialectical advance from individual bad faith and from bad faith relations with others.

The third set of questions concerns Sartre's relativism with respect to choosing values and the futility of actions. For a Sartrean ethics of authenticity to be viable, it must be able to meet the challenges raised against relativism and the special problem presented by the futility even of authentic actions, as recognized by Sartre. If an individual chooses his or her values and sustains them in existence, must that individual not reaffirm previously chosen values before he or she can act on those values—with the consequence that the individual must always reaffirm and can never act, thus becoming Kierkegaard's "hypothetical man"? How can individuals become aware of the fact that they alone must choose values yet adhere to values that are particularly demanding? Finally, how can authentic individuals continue to act while remaining "haunted," as Sartre says, by what they acknowledge to be impossible: coincidence with themselves, with their values, and with others?

In Chapter 5 I develop these questions as they have been raised or answered by Kierkegaard, Stace, and Kant. *Play* will be presented as Sartre's answer; the authentic individual must adopt a nonserious, nonpossessive attitude, which Sartre illuminates by discussing nonappropriative or at least minimally appropriative forms of play. The problems of indecisiveness and futility remain for the serious but not for those who are authentic.

Fourth, Marxists and non-Marxists alike condemn Sartre for what looks like a halfhearted endorsement of Marxism. Whereas Marx ascribes alienation to capitalistic institutions, Sartre argues that alienation cannot be overcome by any revolution; a complete overcoming of alienation is no more possible for groups than for individuals. Whereas non-Marxists frequently propose that alienation is inevitable and revolution therefore futile, Sartre endorses revolution, maintaining that some alienation is avoidable, that scarcity and its attendant forms of social and individual alienation can and should be overcome.

In the sixth chapter, I argue that Sartre can condemn societies as well as individuals because not all alienation is inevitable. Societies and individuals impose avoidable alienation on themselves and on others, and they may strive to overcome it. Even though they fail to overcome all alienation, they nonetheless win by overcoming avoidable alienation and effecting, if only momentarily, the unification toward which they strive.

Finally, are authentic relationships with others possible? If so, what would such relationships be like? Are authentic individuals condemned to an individualism that cuts them off from anything other than superficial contact with others? Chapter 7 develops, largely on the basis of Sartre's literary work, a serious alternative to sequestration and individualism. In Sartre's writings are found instances of interpersonal relationships that exhibit respect for freedom and individuality. Although the participants may strive for a coincidence and a perfect confidence that cannot be attained, sometimes they momentarily overcome alienation and separation in the joyful recognition of freedom and a feeling of harmony with each other.

With these answers to questions raised both by Sartre's philosophy and by traditional ethicists, a Sartrean ethics of authenticity becomes tenable and viable in a way most critics have not recognized. It is reasonable to question, however, whether Sartre would have accepted these answers as consistent with the ethics he promised but did not publish. Although I have based my claims, first and foremost, on work published by Sartre himself, I find considerable support for these claims in *Cahiers pour une morale,* one of apparently several Sartrean manuscripts dealing with ethics and the first such work to be published posthumously. I shall indicate that support at appropriate points in subsequent chapters, using my own translations, which I hope reflect adequately the spirit of the text. Any later, posthumously published manuscripts will require study; their differences from one another will have to be unraveled and, following the method I have used in this study, their ideas considered alongside one another as well as along with the rest of Sartre's work.

An adequate Sartrean ethics must emerge from careful analysis of various of Sartre's works written over a lifetime. Without trying to force conflicting ideas into false harmony, we must try to look below surface incompatibilities for possible reconciliations of conflict. Philosophical reputations have been made by showing Sartre to be a wildly inconsistent thinker—sometimes by reading him superficially, sometimes by taking what he says out of context, sometimes, as Sartre himself observes, by stopping "too soon" and not following the "evolution" of his philosophical thought. He thought it "odd" that critics studied him in this way.[14] Such critics may reject Sartre, but they do not thereby transcend Sartre's thought if Francis Jeanson is right, as I believe he is, that "[to] be liberated from a philosophy, one must at least have tried to make it his own."[15]

2

Human Being and Bad Faith

What men have in common is not a
"nature" but a condition, that is, an
ensemble of limits and restrictions:
the inevitability of death, the
necessity of working for a living, of
living in a world already
inhabited by other men.
    —Sartre, *Anti-Semite and Jew*

Sartre's Ontology

In *Being and Nothingness*, as the book's subtitle indicates, Sartre develops a "phenomenological ontology." His phenomenological ontology is one of being and nothingness, and this seems to connect his phenomenology with that of G. W. F. Hegel. At the same time Sartre explicitly connects his phenomenological method with that of Edmund Husserl. Although Sartre departs early and drastically from the ontological neutrality of Husserl's method, like Husserl, he is concerned with taking a fresh look at experience, with examining and describing it, and with seeing to what it commits us.

Sartre's relation to Hegel goes considerably beyond the superficial dichotomy of "being" and "nothingness." The relationships Sartre develops between these—between being-in-itself *(en-soi)* and being-for-itself *(pour-soi)*—are reminiscent of Hegelian dialectic at least to the extent of there being a movement of opposition and of there being attempts to overcome the oppositions that arise. Being-for-itself, the *pour-soi*, is, according to Sartre, primarily a matter of negating; it separates itself from the fullness of being-in-itself, the *en-soi*. The freedom of being-for-itself lies in its ability to negate. Sartre calls attention to this ability by his use of the word *nothingness* and by his denial of an essence to this being-for-itself. Being-for-itself, then, is a nothingness or a "nothinging," in this particular sense of separating itself from being-in-itself; it desires the fullness that it lacks. This desire, which Sartre calls the desire to be God, plays a crucial role in Sartre's analyses of bad faith and inauthentic relations with others.

The project to be God is doomed to failure since, Sartre argues, God is impossible. It is the project of the being-for-itself to overcome its separation and alienation from being-in-itself, to "metamorphose its own For-itself into an In-itself-For-itself and a project of the appropriation of the world as a totality of being-in-itself." To the extent that man is this desire to be God, man is a "useless passion."[1] Even so, Sartre is concerned to relate the regions of being-in-itself and being-for-itself "which *in theory* are without communication."[2]

Having criticized both idealism and realism as failing to explain the relation between these two regions, Sartre presents a strange combination of realism and idealism. According to Sartre, being-for-itself is consciousness; it creates the *meaning* of phenomena but not the *being* of phenomena. The latter, the being of phenomena, Sartre designates by the term "*en-soi*," or "being-in-itself." Maurice Natanson refers to Sartre's placing being-for-itself at the core of existence as a

"Copernican revolution" at the ontological level. He contrasts Sartre's Copernican revolution with the Copernican revolution effected by Immanuel Kant: Sartre's revolution involves a being-for-itself which is in perpetual flux with consequent and corresponding change in the significations it creates. According to Natanson, what results is an ongoing process, a Copernican revolution that is not complete and that cannot be completed.[3]

Human Being

A human being exists as an uneasy tension between the two regions of being: the for-itself and the in-itself. As consciousnesses that are embodied, human beings relate in themselves the two regions "which in theory are without communication." Although Sartre realizes it is not possible to derive imperatives from ontology's indicatives, nevertheless he thinks that ontology allows us "to catch a glimpse of what sort of ethics will assume its responsibilities when confronted with a *human reality in situation.*"[4] Thus understanding what ethics and morality are, and what they can be, requires considerable clarity about what it is to be human.

According to Sartre, consciousness, being-for-itself, is defined by its intentionality, by the fact that it is consciousness *of* an object. This means that consciousness is necessarily a *positing* of a transcendent object, that "it transcends itself in order to reach an object" and is exhausted in this very positing.[5] At the same time, this consciousness must be conscious of itself. The awareness consciousness always has of itself is nonreflective and nonpositional. Sartre refers to this self-consciousness as consciousness (of) self, in order to make the point that such consciousness of self is not dual and to distinguish it from positional acts of consciousness in which there is duality. It is on the basis of such prereflective consciousness (of) itself that consciousness is able to become reflectively aware of itself and its acts. Thus all consciousness is, at the same time, both consciousness *of* an object and consciousness (of) itself. That all consciousness is consciousness (of) itself entails what Sartre refers to as the "total translucency of consciousness."[6]

On the other hand, there is the being of the in-itself. This being follows, according to Sartre, from an analysis of consciousness. Sartre designates this analysis the "ontological proof." Like Anselm's ontological argument, Sartre's ontological proof moves from consciousness to a being that is not consciousness: all consciousness is intentional and therefore consciousness *of* something which is not consciousness since "to be consciousness *of* something is to be confronted with a concrete and full presence which *is not consciousness.*"[7]

Whereas consciousness is empty (as consciousness *of* an object that exhausts itself in this positing of a transcendent object) and translucent to itself (as consciousness (of) itself), being-in-itself "is opaque to itself precisely because it is filled with itself." This opaque being *is what it is*; "[i]t is full positivity [—i]t knows no otherness."[8] It is superfluous *(de trop)*: "Uncreated, without reason for being, without any connection with another being, being-in-itself is *de trop* for eternity."[9]

Although the regions of for-itself and in-itself are, as Sartre says, "radically separated regions," nonetheless they are ambiguously connected in man.[10] To be human is to be conscious and thus for-itself. Because consciousness necessarily posits objects and exhausts itself in this positing, human consciousness must itself always be directed toward objects, hence toward the in-itself. Owing to the fact of embodiment, however, there is an even more vital tie with being-in-itself. The human individual is an embodied consciousness; thus it is what it is not and is not what it is.

This essential ambiguity of human being is clarified by Sartre with the aid of three sets of properties: facticity and transcendence, being-for-others and being-for-itself, and being-in-the-midst-of-the-world and being-in-the-world. The first pair of properties is facticity and transcendence. Facticity, in general, is the "perpetually evanescent contingency of the in-itself which, without even allowing itself to be apprehended, haunts the for-itself and reattaches it to being-in-itself."[11] One's facticity includes one's body and its limitations, one's birth, education, class, and so on. The individual human being is all of these, yet at the same time, he or she always transcends them by virtue of being able, at least, to interpret them, to take an attitude toward each factor in turn. One is one's facticity in the mode of being what one is not.

The individual, as well as being what it is not and not being what it is, is being-for-others and being-for-itself. A human being's conduct can be looked at from two points of view: his or her own and that of others. These two points of view—or "looks"—may be disparate, and the disparity cannot be resolved by saying that one point of view is reality, whereas the other is mere appearance, only a deformed image of oneself. These two aspects possess an "equal dignity of being."[12] One simply is the ambiguous being that is being-for-others and being-for-itself.

The third double property is that of being-in-the-midst-of-the-world and being-in-the-world. An individual is an "inert presence as a passive object among other objects" (a being-in-the-midst-of-the-world). At the same time, the individual is the "being which causes there to be a world by projecting itself beyond the world toward its own possibilities" (being-in-the-world).[13]

As a being that is what it is not and is not what it is, a human being is facticity and transcendence, being-for-others and being-for-itself, and being-in-the-midst-of-the-world and being-in-the-world. Being human is thus an uneasy tension of opposites, an ambiguous existent. In *Cahiers*, Sartre expresses the ambiguity somewhat differently but again in such a way that this tension is clearly affirmed: "I am *on the same plane* specific object and free subject but never the two at the same time and always the one haunted by the Other."[14]

This recognition of ambiguity is ignored or forgotten by those of Sartre's critics who view Sartrean freedom as absolute, subjective, and isolated. Even Maurice Merleau-Ponty makes this fundamental mistake when he speaks of Sartre as a "good Cartesian" and of Sartre's view as the "Philosophy of the pure subject."[15] These critics usually marvel, with Marcuse, at Sartre's later Marxian "conversion," claiming that Sartre's later emphasis on society's restrictions on human freedom requires a view of embodiment and being-in-the-world totally at odds with his earlier "existentialism."[16]

Sartre himself is prone to overstatement in many of his claims about freedom, sometimes seeming to ignore or reject important qualifications he at other times is so careful to enunciate. Although Sartre thus bears some responsibility for many of the most common misconceptions of his view of freedom, the extent to which he explicitly argued against these, from early to late in his career, must be noted.

Bad Faith, Good Faith, and Authenticity

Human reality as a being that is what it is not and is not what it is connects the two regions of being: being-in-itself and being-for-itself. Because it does so in an ambiguous way—as an uneasy tension of opposites—being human is itself a challenge many would prefer to avoid. To be human is to be free and responsible, even to the point of taking upon oneself one's own birth and bodily infirmities—factors over which, in a sense, one has no control, yet over which one has the important power of interpreting, of giving a significance to, of accepting or rejecting. Responsibility extends even to the way in which one is seen by others and to one's being as an inert presence in the world.

This view of human freedom and its consequent responsibility is an uncompromising one that invalidates most alibis and excuses. That is why Sartre refers to the recognition of our freedom and responsibility as "anguish." It is a recognition many would prefer to avoid and from which they seek an escape. Such avoidance and escape is the goal of bad faith. In bad faith, individuals try not to acknowledge the extent of their freedom and responsibility. They reject the ambiguity of their existence and attempt to resolve the uneasy tension between facticity and transcendence, being-for-others and being-for-itself, and being-in-the-midst-of-the-world and being-in-the-world. Bad faith is the attempt both to establish a relation of identity between the two regions of being and to deny the ambiguous connection that already exists and is at least minimally recognized to exist between them.

Bad faith evinces the same vicious circle as does the attempt (discussed by Sartre in *Cahiers*) to define the species. In the attempt to define the species, the de-

32

finer is always, as a matter of principle, situated outside the definition into which that same definer is
inserted as what is being defined.[17] Similarly, in bad
faith, individuals who try to define themselves solely
in terms of their facticity, being for others, and being-
in-the-midst-of-the-world, by their very attempt
evince the transcendence, being-for-itself, and being-
in-the-world that inevitably remain outside their defi-
nitions while purportedly being included in them.

Thus bad faith is a matter of lying to oneself. Sartre
notes that it is not difficult to understand a lie when
there is in fact another whom the liar intends to deceive and from whom the liar exists as hidden. The
problem in understanding bad faith is that in bad faith
no such duality exists between the liar and the one to
be duped. Because bad faith is a lie to oneself, one in
bad faith must play both parts—deceiver and deceived.
It follows that the same individual as deceiver must
know the truth to be hidden from herself or himself as
the deceived. As Sartre points out, "I must know the
truth very exactly *in order* to conceal it more carefully."[18]

This difficulty in understanding bad faith is com-
pounded by the recognition of the total translucency of
consciousness. Since all consciousness is a consciousness (of) itself, this must hold as well for the consciousness in bad faith; in other words, one must be
conscious (of) one's bad faith. At the same time, this
presents a problem: if one is aware of what one is
doing, then one could hardly succeed in what one
is trying to do—namely, deceive oneself. Thus Sartre is
forced to distinguish bad faith from cynicism. If, according to Sartre, "I deliberately and cynically attempt
to lie to myself, I fail completely in this undertaking;
the lie falls back and collapses beneath my look; it is

ruined *from behind* by the very consciousness of lying to myself which pitilessly constitutes itself well within my project as its very condition."[19]

Herbert Fingarette's account of self-deception parallels that of Sartre at this point, nicely illuminating what transpires in bad faith. Fingarette agrees with Sartre that self-deception is not cynical; rather, as he points out, it is almost sincere: those who deceive themselves tell others the same stories about what they are doing as they tell themselves, and this is "a distinctive mark of sincerity."[20] Yet this is a qualified sincerity; the apparent sincerity of such an individual conflicts with the fact that "we observe that in other respects he shows convincing signs of being engaged in the way we ascribe to him but which he sincerely denies. The purposefulness and the often remarkable ingenuity with which he carries through the engagement lead us to insist that 'He must know what he is doing; he *must* know the truth.'"[21] Although the self-deceiver "spells things out to others as he does to himself, and . . . is not unintentionally wrong in the way he spells things out to himself [, n]evertheless he does not spell them out to himself as they are."[22] The way he spells things out both to others and to himself is purposely wrong.

Bad faith, as opposed to cynicism, is a kind of psychic structure which Sartre calls "metastable." According to Hazel Barnes, the translator of *Being and Nothingness*, this means that this structure is "subject to sudden changes or transitions,"[23] although, as Sartre himself says, "it presents nonetheless an autonomous and durable form."[24] Although, in continually vacillating between good faith and cynicism, bad faith shares with cynicism an evanescence, it nevertheless is such that one can live in bad faith.[25] "One *puts oneself* in bad faith as one goes to sleep and one is in bad faith as one dreams."[26] As Fingarette observes, this analogy with sleep and dreams is particularly helpful: "When one puts oneself to sleep one acts with purpose, but part of the skill consists finally in avoiding reflection upon one's purpose."[27] Bad faith, then, is not cynical; it escapes the collapse that inevitably would follow the cynical attempt to lie to oneself.

There remains the problem of understanding bad faith without introducing the duality of deceiver and deceived into consciousness itself. Recourse to the unconscious is the escape taken in the psychoanalytic interpretation of bad faith. As Sartre sees it, the id and the ego of psychoanalysis introduce into consciousness itself the duality of *myself* and *another*, and that "places me in the same relation to myself that the Other is in with respect to me."[28] It thus becomes impossible to understand the resistance (noted by Freud) on the part of the patient as the analyst approaches the truth concerning the patient's problem or problems. Such resistance can be understood only if the censor is actually "consciousness (of) being conscious of the drive to be repressed, but precisely *in order not to be conscious of it.*" Thus Freudian analysis does not aid in the understanding of bad faith, since it at best merely localizes "this double activity of repulsion and attraction on the level of the censor."[29]

Sartre turns to a description of patterns of bad faith to show how bad faith can be understood on the basis of the recognition of man as a being that is what it is not and is not what it is. His first example is that of a woman who goes out for the first time with a particular man. She knows quite well the intentions of her companion, but she does not wish to make a decision with respect to these, partly because she does not know what she wants. On the one hand, she is well aware of the desire she inspires but would, as Sartre presents her, be horrified and humiliated by the desire in its cruelty and nakedness. On the other hand, she is not interested in a respect that would be merely respect. She thus desires a feeling addressed wholly to her personality—to her freedom—and which recognizes her freedom, but which is at the same time wholly desire, addressed wholly to her body as object.[30]

In developing this example, Sartre asks what would happen if the man takes the woman's hand. This presents her with an immediate problem, since she wants to postpone as long as possible making a decision. By taking her hand, her companion calls for an immediate decision and thus risks changing the situation. This challenge, Sartre tells us, is "met" by the woman's not "noticing" her hand left in the hand of her companion. She fails to notice by becoming for the moment all intellect, a personality, a consciousness. She divorces herself from her body by drawing her companion into a lofty and sentimental discussion of "Life" and of her life in particular. Thus the hand she leaves "between the warm hands of her companion" is neither consenting to nor resisting his advances; it can neither consent nor resist, since it is a mere thing.[31]

Another example is that of a waiter in a cafe. Sartre describes his movement as being a bit too precise, a bit too rapid, bending forward a bit too eagerly. Through his voice and his eyes, the waiter expresses an interest somewhat too solicitous of the customer's tastes. As he walks, he tries to imitate the "inflexible stiffness of some kind of automaton" while at the same time "carrying his tray with the recklessness of a tightrope-walker." Thus the waiter plays at being a waiter; he attempts thereby to *realize* his condition, to realize a "being-in-itself of the cafe waiter." In trying to *be* a cafe waiter, he tries to act as though he is not the source of the value and urgency of his duties and the rights of his position, as though he did not freely choose to get up each morning at five and to sustain in existence his role as waiter.[32]

Arthur C. Danto criticizes this and other examples offered by Sartre, inasmuch as Sartre fails to establish that the waiter and others are aware of their freedom. If individuals are not aware of their freedom, Danto argues, they may be wrong in what they assume or believe about values, but they will not be in bad faith. If, as Danto believes, anguish, the awareness of freedom, is exceptional and generally not found in human beings, then it is incumbent upon Sartre to establish at the outset that each person in his examples is sufficiently aware of his or her freedom.[33] Sartre would probably reject such a burden of proof, agreeing instead with de Beauvoir, that, whereas children may live in a world of ready-made values they have not helped to establish, it is "very rare" for such an infantile lack of awareness to extend beyond adolescence.[34]

Another aspect of the waiter example has been recognized but misinterpreted by D. Z. Phillips.[35] Sartre does say that society imposes an "obligation" on waiters, and indeed on all tradesmen, since: "A grocer who dreams is offensive to the buyer, because such a grocer is not wholly a grocer." Thus "[society] demands that he limit himself to his function as a grocer." In response to society's demand, "there is the dance of the grocer, of the tailor, of the auctioneer, by which they endeavor to persuade their clientele that they are nothing but a grocer, an auctioneer, and tailor."[36] Phillips interprets this to mean that all waiters are in bad faith. He seems to miss his own crucial distinction between an "obligation imposed from without" on the waiter and his part in the ceremony "[from] the inside, from the point of view of the waiter."[37] To the extent

37

that the one who assumes the role is free to do *anything* else—including simply defying the expectations placed on those in that role—that one is never identical to the role. Those who try to convince themselves of such identity role are in bad faith—this is just an attempt at self-deception. To the extent that society demands such identification from individuals in these roles, however, there is something tantamount to bad faith in society's very structuring of the roles. This may make it extremely difficult for anyone in these roles to escape bad faith; but such recognition that social structures limit human freedom and impede authenticity is less an indictment of individual waiters than an early recognition by Sartre of the way in which social constructions curtail individual freedom. Herein, as Thomas R. Flynn recognizes, is "an awareness of social issues in *Being and Nothingness* overlooked by the majority of Sartre's commentators."[38]

A detailed account of the relationship of society to the individual was undertaken by Sartre in his *Critique of Dialectical Reason* (analyzed in Chapter 5). Here, we need only observe that Sartre's waiter makes evident both the precariousness and the inescapability of human freedom. It is not the absolute freedom ascribed to Sartre by Marcuse and many others, the unalterable and truly inalienable "inner" or "metaphysical" freedom Sartre himself so clearly rejects, but, rather, a freedom such that the "free man" can hope for liberation inasmuch as "he is not free and bound in respect to the same things."[39] To say that the victim of torture or oppression is free is not to blame the victim for her or his situation, as do some who have tried to apply existentialism to psychotherapy; neither is it to justify the status quo and thereby relieve torturers and oppressors of their responsibility. Rather, it is to recognize that even though torture or oppression may leave individuals "no choice other than resignation or revolution," such severely curtailed choices nonetheless manifest the victim's freedom to choose.[40]

According to Sartre, what the examples of the woman and the waiter reveal about bad faith is that bad faith is a matter of forming contradictory concepts. It makes use of the double property of facticity and transcendence. The woman uses this double property in several ways. First, she disarms the actions of her companion by reducing them to their facticity—to existing only in the mode of the in-itself. At the same time, she recognizes only the transcendence of his desire—its not being what it is—and to this extent allows herself to enjoy the desire. Third, she realizes herself as pure consciousness, as not being her own body, and contemplates her body as though it were merely a passive object, a thing, which neither provokes nor avoids the events that simply *happen* to it.[41]

The waiter, too, makes use of this double property of facticity and transcendence in his playing at *being* a waiter. The waiter's facticity can be seen in his very situation; his situation is in fact the situation appropriate to a cafe waiter: he *does* get up at five, go to the restaurant, set up, and wait on customers. Although one must play a role, play, for example, at being a waiter in order to be one, still, as Sartre recognizes, it would be singularly futile, given the condition of the waiter, for him to play at being a diplomat or a sailor.[42] What characterizes the waiter in bad faith is that he tries to ignore the fact that he is free with respect to constituting the meaning of his situation; he tries to deny and hide from himself his transcendence of the meaning he has given to his situation by virtue of the fact that, by his actions, he sustains this role in existence.

This is one type of bad faith, a type that utilizes the double property of facticity and transcendence. Bad faith does not seek to effect the valid albeit ambiguous coordination of which these aspects of a human being are and ought to be capable; on the contrary, bad faith seeks only to affirm the identity of these while preserving their differences. It thereby affirms "facticity as *being* transcendence and transcendence as *being* facticity, in such a way that at the instant when a person apprehends the one, he can find himself abruptly faced with the other."[43]

In characterizing this move as bad faith, Sartre affirms freedom as an aspect of human existence *and* as something to be accomplished, advocating a "type of project which has freedom for its foundation and its goal."[44] As Jeanson points out,

> Sartre's "freedom" simply refers to human freedom as opposed to the determinism of the thing. However, this freedom to which we are "condemned" must be made *our own* or else it will too soon appear as yet another determinism. We *are* free, but this in no way relieves us from having to *make* ourselves free. First, ontology has only to tell us whether such an endeavor has a meaning. It does have a meaning, one that is wholly negative, since *essentially* we are not determined. It remains for us to give it a positive meaning in the practical attitude. We determine ourselves *existentially*, through the practical attitude, drawing support from the very difficulties inherent in our presence in the world.[45]

Thus, as Robert V. Stone observes in his introduction to his translation of Jeanson's work, Jeanson recognizes in Sartre a "distinction between a 'natural' or unreflective freedom evinced in our alienations—which is the object of ontological description—and a 'freedom-as-valued' in which freedom is recovered and practiced as the explicit objective of a reflective moral attitude."[46] Clearly, Sartre has denounced as bad faith any attempt to absorb facticity into freedom or freedom into facticity. His freedom is neither absolute as Marcuse and sometimes Merleau-Ponty claim, nor the "ready-made freedom" (as facticity) that Merleau-Ponty at other times ascribes to Sartre.[47]

Other types of bad faith as well are made possible by the ambiguity of human being. Not only is the human being at once a facticity and a transcendence, but it is also a being-for-itself and a being-for-others. To become aware of one's being-for-others is to become aware of one's object-side. This is a side of himself of which, in Sartre's example, the jealous man at the keyhole is unaware as he watches the scene unfolding on the other side of the door. A footstep in the hall makes him aware that he has been seen by someone else. He becomes aware of the self he already was—but "without knowing it."[48] This is so even if the footstep in the hall was that of a blind person or of an individual totally absorbed in his or her own thoughts and who fails to see the jealous man at the keyhole. It is so even if the apparent footstep turns out to have been only the creaking of the floor.

Any conduct can be seen from each of two points of view—that of the agent and that of another. Neither of these possibly quite disparate views is reality and the other mere appearance; neither can be discounted as merely a deformed image of the agent. Nonetheless, an individual may seek to use one as reality in order to escape from the other, which is then treated as mere appearance. The "equal dignity of being" possessed by the two aspects enables one to establish a "perpetual game of escape from the for-itself to the for-others and from the for-others to the for-itself."[49]

41

An individual who prays furnishes a slightly different example of this type of bad faith, an example developed in *Cahiers*. Such an individual evinces the following contradiction: "In accepting and by my acceptance, I wish to obtain the opposite of what I accept. I submit myself to that which I don't want in order that the Master might wish what I do want." In prayer, the individual identifies with her or his impotence (the individual's being-for-others) and, in a move opposite to desire, gives herself or himself over "to a freedom as a vassal gives himself to his lord."[50]

A final duplicity derived from human reality and utilized by bad faith is that of being-in-the-midst-of-the-world and being-in-the-world. Sartre sees this double aspect as having been used in the example of the woman and her would-be lover. The woman made use of her being-in-the-midst-of-the-world in order to avoid and relieve herself of the possibilities of her being-in-the-world. Thus she tried to be an "inert presence," a passive object among other objects, to escape being that which "causes there to be a world by projecting itself beyond the world toward its possibilities."[51]

Thus human reality's being what it is not and not being what it is provides a condition for the possibility of bad faith. Bad faith plays on the double properties of this being—facticity and transcendence, being-for-others and being-for-itself, being-in-the-midst-of-the-world and being-in-the-world—and in each case attempts to subsume one under the other, with nothing left over.

Paradoxically, even good faith is for Sartre a matter of bad faith. Sartre's example of the homosexual and his critic—"the champion of sincerity"—makes this point. A homosexual may be in bad faith by refusing to recognize himself as a homosexual even though he recognizes his inclination and avows each homosexual

42

act which he has performed. While admitting his "faults," such a homosexual in part (and quite properly) resists "the crushing view that his mistakes constitute for him a destiny." It is precisely in this way that the champion of sincerity or of good faith demands that the homosexual recognize himself: the critic urges the homosexual to identify himself as a thing—"to be what he is in order no longer to be what he is."[52] The sincere man, as much as the one in bad faith, is trying not to be what he is; only his method differs. He attempts to constitute himself as what he is in order not to be this. In confessing that he is evil, he exchanges "his disturbing 'freedom for evil'" for "an inanimate character of evil," but at the same time escapes being an evil thing by virtue of the fact that he confesses, that he contemplates his being evil and thus asserts his freedom either to maintain it or to let it collapse.[53]

The problem with both bad and good faith is that they are matters of *faith*. According to Sartre, faith or belief involves "the adherence of being to its object when the object is not given or is given indistinctly."[54] Since all consciousness is consciousness (of) being conscious, believing must itself be consciousness (of) believing. Thus believing carries the seeds of its own undoing within itself, since, at least potentially, it involves knowing that one believes. Knowing that one believes, however, one no longer believes: the confidence essential to faith is destroyed as soon as one becomes aware that it is merely faith, that the object believed in is not given or is given indistinctly. Belief, then, "is a being which questions its own being, which can realize itself only in its destruction, which can manifest itself to itself only by denying itself."[55]

Bad faith uses this self-destruction within all faith. The project of bad faith is, first of all, a decision on the nature of truth. Rejecting the "norms and criteria of truth as they are accepted by the critical thought of good faith," bad faith accepts "a peculiar type of evidence"—"*non-persuasive* evidence"—and in advance resigns itself to not being persuaded, to not being fulfilled by this evidence. This decision is, Sartre says, "a spontaneous determination of our being," not the reflective voluntary decision of cynicism.[56] Thus bad faith uses the self-destruction inherent in all belief. Belief always falls short; one can never wholly believe what one believes. Therefore, since no belief is possible, bad faith makes room for every impossible belief. Sartre illustrates this view with the example of believing oneself courageous: "My inability to *believe* that I am courageous will not discourage me since every belief involves not quite believing. I shall define this impossible belief as *my* belief."[57]

At the same time that bad faith makes use of the self-destruction inherent in all faith, it must defend itself from the demands of good faith, even though these have been disarmed in advance by virtue of their being only matters of "faith." Bad faith uses the double-aspect properties of the human being to defend itself from these demands. Continuing the example of wishing to believe oneself courageous, Sartre notes that the knowledge that one is a coward threatens to destroy one's belief. In bad faith, however, one observes that in the mode of being-in-itself, one is no more courageous than one is cowardly. Bad faith thus attempts to "flee what it cannot flee, to flee what it is. The very project of flight reveals to bad faith an inner disintegration which bad faith wishes to be."[58]

On the one hand, therefore, bad faith seeks to escape what one is by means of not-being-what-one-is.[59] Bad faith denies its bad faith and denies the in-itself that it is not (in the mode of not being what one is) but denies this in the mode of not being what one is not. Good faith, on the other hand, seeks to flee itself in the other direction—that of the in-itself it should be but is not. Thus both good and bad faith play off one part of the definition of man against the other. Both try to introduce into the being of man a principle that is straightforwardly applicable only to the in-itself—the principle of identity.[60]

Both good and bad faith are corruptions of being. The "self-recovery" of this previously corrupted being is "authenticity." Although Sartre continually postponed a thorough discussion of this notion, or at least the publication of such discussion, there is some indication in the patterns of bad faith themselves of what authenticity would involve. When Sartre discusses the bad faith of the homosexual in his example, he notes that the homosexual plays on the word *being*, but that he would be right if he simply denied being a homosexual in the sense of not being what he is. In other words, he would be correct if, in acknowledging his past conduct as the conduct of a homosexual, he recognizes that to that extent he is a homosexual while also recognizing that he is his past in the mode of not being it, that he is not exhaustively so characterized.[61] Whether his sexual preference itself is freely chosen or is a part of his facticity does not matter. Whichever is the case, he must assume responsibility for the preference, at least in the sense of his attitudes toward and interpretations of this preference, and for any actions undertaken on the basis of this preference. That is to say, he would be right if he recognized himself as a being that is what it is not and is not what it is.

An authentic individual recognizes the ambiguity of the human situation. Those in bad faith tend to deny this ambiguity by postulating as absolute only one side of the ambiguity, thereby denying the other. Authenticity, therefore, is the recovery—the awareness and acceptance of—this basic ambiguity: "Authenticity, it is almost needless to say, consists in having a true and lucid consciousness of the situation, in assuming the responsibilities and risks that it involves, in accepting it in pride or humiliation, sometimes in horror or hate."[62] In *Cahiers,* an early work on ethics which Sartre decided not to publish, conversion (and thus authenticity) is connected with the renouncing of appropriation:

> the conversion consists of renouncing the category of *appropriation,* which is able to control only the relations of the For-itself with things, in order to introduce in the internal relation of the Person the relation of *solidarity,* which will be much later transformed into solidarity with others. In refusing to possess the reflected, it unveils the unappropriable character of reflected experience *(Erlebnis).* But at the same time it creates a type of unity special to the existent, and this is the *moral* unity in reference to and in contractual accord with itself. This unity is willed. Sincerity is therefore excluded because it bears on that which I *am.* Authenticity bears on what I will. . . . Pure and authentic reflection is a will for that which I will.[63]

In affirming the fundamental ambiguity of human existence, Sartre escapes the total voluntarism into which many of his critics try to force him. Alasdair MacIntyre is representative of these critics when he depicts Sartre's self as a "self that can have no history."[64] Sartre's view, in fact, is far closer to MacIntyre's than the latter recognizes. With his emphasis on the individual's facticity, past, and the way that person is seen by others, Sartre, like MacIntyre, acknowledges that each person has a history of which others are part. The individual who chooses values and who chooses himself or herself through such value choices is embodied and is historically and socially situated. Bodily, historical, and social factors affect the range of choices available to any individual, as Sartre clearly observed in the case of the waiter. Sartre simply emphasizes (as MacIntyre does not) the way these stories remain fluid as long as the individuals are alive. With each decision, the individual may drastically alter the story to the extent that it involves more than a recounting of brute, uninterpreted, and valueless facts. The interpretation of one's past and situation may thereby be changed, although this process leaves standing (can never abolish) the events and facts themselves.

3

Lying to Oneself

Man cannot will unless he has first
understood that he can count on
nothing but himself: that he is
alone, left alone on earth in the
middle of his infinite
responsibilities, with neither help
nor succor, with no other goal but
the one he will set for himself, with
no other destiny but the one he will
forge on this earth.
—Sartre, "A More Precise
Characterization of
Existentialism"

Critics of existentialism—from traditional Christians, to those writing for the popular press, to the most radical Marxists—have maintained that Sartre's existentialism leaves him unable to judge morally the actions of others. In his early tract "Existentialism is a Humanism," Sartre addressed a diverse and not overly philosophy-oriented audience and defended himself from the accusation that, as an existentialist, he was unable to judge others.[1] On the contrary, he claimed that, as a consistent existentialist, he was able to make two different judgments on the actions of another person.

There is, first, the possibility of making a "logical

judgment" on the actions of another. This judgment, Sartre affirmed, concerns the actions of those who attempt to deceive themselves about their freedom: "Since we have defined the situation of man as one of free choice, without excuse and without help, any man who takes refuge behind the excuse of his passions, or by inventing some deterministic doctrine, is a self-deceiver."[2] According to Sartre, this is merely a logical judgment and nothing more. Both propositions involved in the individual's situation simply cannot be true. This judgment is no more than a straightforward recognition of the inconsistency of the self-deceiver.

Those who affirm the "situation of man as one of free choice, without excuse and without help" may, in addition to a logical judgment, make a "moral judgment" on the actions of another. Where the logical judgment only acknowledged that an individual "who takes refuge behind the excuse of his passions, or by inventing some deterministic doctrine" is deceiving herself or himself, the moral judgment proclaims that the individual *should not* do this. Sartre bases the possibility of this moral judgment on what he recognizes as fact, namely, that freedom is the foundation of all values: "For I declare that freedom, in respect of concrete circumstances, can have no other end and aim but itself; and when once a man has seen that values depend upon himself, in that state of forsakenness he can will only one thing, and that is freedom as the foundation of all values."[3]

Moreover, for Sartre, it is not enough for individuals merely to will their own freedom; they must will the freedom of others as well. In willing freedom for freedom's sake "in and through particular circumstances," we discover that freedom "depends entirely upon the freedom of others and that the freedom of others depends upon our own."[4] In 1949, replying to an attack by Georges Lukács, Sartre made this point in a slightly different way: "if I take my own freedom as my goal, it involves requiring all the others to be free. In the choice I make of my freedom, the freedom of the others is demanded."[5]

How is Sartre's support in "Existentialism is a Humanism" for the making of moral judgments on the actions of others to be interpreted? This question is especially perplexing, inasmuch as in the same work, Sartre claimed both that "everything is indeed permitted if God does not exist" and that God does not exist.[6] If Sartre concludes (as he must) from these claims that "everything is indeed permitted," how can he go on to make moral judgments concerning the actions of others?

Human beings are described by Sartre as totally free and as creators of their values. Admittedly Sartre's claims refer to himself as well as to others; Sartre himself must be recognized as totally free and as a creator of values. In this sense surely there is no difficulty in allowing that Sartre can no more avoid making moral judgments than can anyone else. But is the moral judgment Sartre justifies in "Existentialism is a Humanism" merely one that he, acting as a free and responsible individual, has chosen to make? Must the rest of us see this moral judgment on those in bad faith, those who deceive themselves concerning their freedom, as arbitrary, simply reflecting the values Sartre himself chose but which we may choose not to share?

Sartre developed his "moral judgment" as following from the tenets of existentialism. He did not present it as merely reflecting his own choice of values, and few if any of his critics have interpreted it that way. Most have viewed his "moral judgment," rather, as an unjustifiable lapse into a Kantian ethics of universalizability when he claims both that in choosing for oneself one chooses for all men and that one cannot but will one's own freedom once one realizes that freedom is the foundation of all values. For these critics, what is unwarranted and unjustifiable about this attempt to make a moral judgment is the allegedly implicit appeal to a reason that somehow is the source of a categorical imperative such as: "Act only on that maxim through which you can at the same time will that it should become a universal law."[7] Truly, Sartre has no basis for such a move. When Iris Murdoch rejects what she takes to be Sartre's endorsement of such Kantianism, she seems correct in objecting that Sartre "does not believe in a Kantian self which is precisely the same in each of us."[8] Moreover, Sartre himself rejects Kantian morality, noting that it merely "offers criteria for isolated actions."[9]

Mary Warnock and others have argued that Sartre's subjectivist position on values undermines the possibility of an ethics, since one never can say that one thing is more valuable than another without assuming objective values and thereby adopting the spirit of seriousness Sartre so abhors.[10] Sartre does seem to maintain that once one realizes that freedom is the foundation of all values, one must, to be consistent, will freedom as itself a value. This appears to presuppose that consistency has some merit preexisting any choice of values by individual human beings. If that is true, then Sartre's recommendation of freedom as a value presupposes an objectivist theory of value—at least one objective value (that of consistency itself)—which he has denied.

Sartre's justification of his moral judgment on the bad faith of others, however, need not be connected with Kant's categorical imperative or with the spirit of seriousness and its theory of objective values. Interpreting Sartre's justification along the lines of Kant's categorical imperative is highly problematic, inasmuch as part of the justification is concerned with an individual's willing freedom as the foundation of all values once it is realized that "freedom, in respect of concrete circumstances, can have no other end and aim but itself." At most, universalization enters into the justification of the additional claim that individuals must also will the freedom of others inasmuch as they discover, in willing freedom for freedom's sake "in and through particular circumstances," that such freedom "depends entirely upon the freedom of others and that the freedom of others depends upon our own."[11]

Although universalization may appear to enter into the justification of this additional claim concerning the willing of the freedom of others, a problem arises in interpreting even this justification in a Kantian way, at least à la Kant's categorical imperative. The problem is that Sartre's argument appears to introduce a means/ end distinction with which a Kantian categorical imperative can hardly be reconciled. In fact, it looks as though Sartre is arguing more along the lines of a hypothetical imperative: since one's freedom—concrete freedom vis-à-vis particular circumstances—is inextricably connected with the freedom of others, one cannot will one's own freedom without willing the freedom of others. Rather than universalizing vis-à-vis the categorical imperative, Sartre's argument can be seen as affirming Kant's recognition, with respect to hypothetical imperatives, that one who wills the end wills the means.[12] This, Kant claims, is purely analytic; if Kant is right here, Sartre's use of such a claim similarly is purely analytic and thus does not necessitate his recognition of a "Kantian self which is precisely the same in each of us." Consequently, as Hazel

E. Barnes recognizes in her book on existential ethics, although Sartre's imperative is reminiscent of Kant's, nevertheless it differs significantly inasmuch as it is hypothetical, not categorical.[13]

This point can be supplemented by a parallel argument found in *What Is Literature?* where Sartre maintains that certain actions, particularly the act of writing, implicate the freedom of others. Thus, he argues, "the writer appeals to the reader's freedom to collaborate in the production of his work." Without such collaboration, the book "falls back and collapses; there remain only ink spots on musty paper." Sartre distinguishes the "moral imperative" that is discerned "at the heart of the aesthetic imperative" from the hypothetical imperative which tools present us. A hammer, for example, is a "congealed outline of an operation," but it may, as Sartre observes, be used "to nail up a case or to hit my neighbor over the head."[14] Or the hammer may not be used at all. It simply offers itself in service to one's freedom. The book, on the other hand, *requires* the reader's freedom rather than serving it. Freedom cannot be constrained, fascinated, or entreated. "There is only one way of attaining it; first, by recognizing it, then, having confidence in it, and finally, requiring of it an act, an act in its own name, that is, in the name of the confidence that one brings to it."[15] Thus the moral imperative incumbent on the writer is one by virtue of which the writer is required to will the freedom of his readers. Once again, one who wills the end wills the means.

It is not just in "Existentialism is a Humanism" that Sartre makes the broader claim that one cannot will one's own freedom without willing that of others; in *Anti-Semite and Jew,* he says: "Anti-Semitism is a problem that affects us all directly; we are all bound to the Jew, because anti-Semitism leads straight to National Socialism. And if we do not respect the person of the Israelite, who will respect us? . . . What must be done is to point out to each one that the fate of the Jews is *his* fate. Not one Frenchman will be free so long as the Jews do not enjoy the fulness of their rights. Not one Frenchman will be secure so long as a single Jew— in France or *in the world at large*—can fear for his life."[16]

In concluding that we should therefore work against oppression, Sartre does not thereby save us from Kantianism only to throw us into the arms of utilitarianism. Inasmuch as it is freedom for which we must work, Sartre rejects the purely quantitative weighing of ways to achieve this freedom. Recognizing that "the end is the synthetic unity of the means employed," he argues: "Thus, there are means which risk destroying the end which they intend to realize because by their mere presence they smash the synthetic unity which they wish to enter." Certain means are therefore to be rejected, not because they are measurably less effective in bringing about their goals but rather because they "introduce a *qualitative* alteration into the end and consequently are not measurable."[17] For example, Sartre asks if it is permissible for a revolutionary party to lie and consequently to "perpetuate oppression with the pretext of putting an end to it." He answers: "Not if it helps to create a *lied-to* and *lying* mankind; for then the men who take power are no longer those who deserve to get hold of it; and the reasons one had for abolishing oppression are undermined by the way he goes about abolishing it."[18]

More generally, violence is to be rejected as a means of establishing a utopia where each treats the other as an end—the kingdom of ends—since "it permits of attaining it [the end] in appearance but . . . ruins it secretly in reality." It is like Sartre's example of rape, which "permits of obtaining *one time* the body of a woman but, if I want to be the real possessor of this body for life or for a long relationship, it ruins that possibility."[19]

Sartre's justification of the claim that one must will freedom as the foundation of all values also can be interpreted as involving the recognition that one who wills the end wills the means. The justification can be seen as developing what Kant would call an apodictic hypothetical imperative. At least for those who become aware that they are free, that values depend on themselves, the willing of their own freedom is in a sense inevitable. In bad faith, individuals may endeavor to deceive themselves about their freedom; nonetheless, in the very effort to flee their freedom and hide behind deterministic excuses, they make choices. By willing, they exercise and thereby, at least implicitly, affirm the very freedom they endeavor to deny. The point is simply that those in self-deception are aware of their freedom and in some sense are aware that they must will this freedom even in their attempt to hide it from themselves. Such individuals can be said not to be willing the means as they attempt to will the end.

There is more here than a conflict within the will. If Sartre is right, this conflict is one that eats away at the heart of the possibility of morality. To be moral, one must be free and must freely choose one's values. Freely choosing values while rejecting one's freedom warrants the moral condemnation of those who freely choose their values *and* who also will the means— their own freedom—regardless of the values chosen. To choose one's own values is to will the means—freedom; thus those who try to choose values without willing their freedom can be condemned, on their own grounds, by a hypothetical imperative of which they claim to accept the specified end but without willing the means. In this way, Sartre offers a foundation for a moral judgment condemning a certain kind of lie, that involved in bad faith. He thereby develops a moral judgment to which all who strive to be moral can subscribe, whatever values they, in their freedom, may choose. In doing so, Sartre offers a single and a singular moral judgment which seems to place a certain kind of lie at the base of immorality.

In his *Treatise of Human Nature*, David Hume condemned a moralist named Wollaston for the latter's attempt to place falsehood as the "foundation of all guilt and moral deformity." For Wollaston, it seems, such an action as a man's "lewd behavior" with a neighbor's wife resembles a lie or falsehood inasmuch as it may cause others mistakenly to take the two for husband and wife. Hume objects that this would mean that vice is avoided if actions go undetected but, more important, that it leaves us unable "to give a reason why truth is virtuous and falsehood vicious."[20]

Without turning to feeling, as did Hume, or even to individual choice, Sartre can condemn the self-deception of bad faith by noting that, in effect, this is an attempt to will the end without willing the means. A hypothetical imperative to which an individual in bad faith implicitly makes a commitment allows us to conclude that that individual should will freedom. To the extent that individuals do not will their own freedom, they are condemned, in a sense, on their own grounds—certainly in the eyes of those who clearly recognize and endorse the demands of morality.

Because freedom stands in a unique position of means to every choice, the choice of anything whatsoever as a value logically entails the choice of freedom as a value. As de Beauvoir argues, "Freedom is the source from which all significations and all values spring. It is the original condition of all justification of existence. The man who seeks to justify his life must want freedom itself absolutely and above everything else. . . . To will oneself moral and to will oneself free are one and the same decision."[21]

If to value anything whatsoever is to value freedom, then it seems unfair to accuse Sartre of importing an objective value—that of consistency—into his ethics. Those who affirm self-contradictions remove themselves from the framework of human communication. It is difficult to see why it is incumbent on Sartre or any ethicist to produce reasons and arguments to convince those who have thus removed themselves from logic and therefore from discourse. Indeed, in *Cahiers*, Sartre specifically argues against such removal of oneself from logic and discourse. There he notes that a theme of violence is present in the refusal of the temporal and the discursive. Thus violence is involved in the ad hominem attack and in the appeal to authority, as well as in the refusal of logic, discourse, and temporality. One who defends a position by refusing all relation with the other—or by refusing temporality, that is, change, a future to his or her thought (presumably refusing to allow oneself to be convinced or to recognize the logical implications of one's own positions)— Sartre says, retires from the human community.[22]

To say that Sartre thereby imports an objective value into his existentialism is to misinterpret Sartre's voluntarism with respect to values. That one must choose one's own values does not give one license to break the rules of logic. Indeed, choosing, like affirming or denying, presupposes the principles of noncontradiction, identity, and the excluded middle. The question, Why should one who chooses the end will the means?, can have no answer except that willing the means is at least part of what is meant by willing the end. Whatever is going on, one who allegedly wills the end without at the same time willing the means is not truly willing the end. To the extent that such individuals affirm to themselves or to others that they are willing an end without willing the means, they in effect condemn their own activity, if not to themselves at least as far as the others are concerned.

To argue, as Sartre does, that those who recognize their own freedom must will their own freedom and that of others is therefore neither to move into a question-begging position like that of Wollaston nor to lapse into an unwarranted and unjustified Kantianism; it is simply to take seriously the demands of morality. Something similar should be said for Sartre's claim that whatever values one chooses, that choice is made for everyone. Rather than interpret this as a dubious appeal to Kant's categorical imperative, one can see this rather as another analytic reading, on Sartre's part, of the demands of morality.

Sartre would be in good company if at this point he were saying not that actions are moral only if they or their maxims are universalizable or can be willed as universal laws but, rather, that values and principles must be universal if they are *moral* values and principles. This too can be seen as an analytic claim; values may indeed be chosen that are not meant to hold for all human beings, but whatever sort of values they are, they simply are not moral values. Kurt Baier makes this point about moral principles when he says: "the point of view of morality . . . must be thought of as a standpoint from which principles are considered as being acted on *by everyone*. Moral principles are not merely principles on which a person must always act without making exceptions, but they are principles *meant for everybody*."[23]

Although Sartre *could* support his claim this way, I can find no evidence that he ever did so. He seems, rather, to emphasize that our actions create an image of the human, as we would have it be. For Sartre, human beings are what they do; there is no independently existing "essence" of the human. We need only to look to individual behavior to see what human beings *can* be and, correlatively, to see what individuals think *should* be. Thus Sartre emphasizes the way in which actions affect the "human" in the agent. For example, in *Cahiers*, he rejects pity not because of the way it diminishes the individual to whom one addresses one's pity but rather because of the way in which this pity directly "overtakes" the pitier: "not as one says, insofar as I put myself, by the imagination, in his place: [but rather] to the extent that it diminishes the human in his person."[24]

Finally, there is in *Cahiers* a justification that appears utilitarian but that nevertheless seems to avoid the obvious pitfalls of a straightforwardly utilitarian appeal in a philosophical position such as Sartre's. In discussing the "appeal," in which I generously and freely manifest my enterprise to the other, in which I will it to the other, Sartre observes that there is here

> acceptance that my operation might not be effected by me alone, that is, acceptance: (1) that the other haunt my realized end, that is, haunt me myself insofar as I must announce what I am by the object (therefore, a beginning of this moral conversion that will consist of preferring that the creation exist as something purely independent and also of resigning myself to lose myself and to alienate myself to the profit of this creation without it, however, ceasing to be conditional); (2) that the other transcends me by all his freedom but *toward my end*.[25]

Here, Sartre makes an appeal that is very much within the strictures delimited by his emphasis on and recommendation of despair—the sense that we must "limit ourselves to a reliance upon that which is within our wills, or within the sum of the probabilities which render our action feasible, . . . that we should act without hope."[26] In accepting my being-for-others, I acknowledge that my acts are to that extent no longer in my power. Moreover, by virtue of having an object-side, I (along with my efforts) am subject to violence.[27] Thus, in willing my end, I must will not just the non-interference but the aid of the other as well, and do what I can to secure that noninterference and aid. Here, Sartre is not judging means by the ends they secure but rather (once again, in the analytic spirit of "whoever wills the end wills the means") saying something about what it means to will any end. Whatever the end, in willing it, a person implicates all others and thereby wills for everyone. In conversations with de Beauvoir during August and September 1974, Sartre, in a similarly analytic spirit, says: "the idea of my liberty implies the idea of the liberty of others."[28]

What about choices and values clearly not meant to hold for everyone? Peter Caws worries that if choosing requires choosing for all (he refers to this as the "generalization argument"), then anyone choosing to be a Jew must choose "at the same time that all men should be Jews." Caws suggests that Sartre drops "his form of the generalization argument" in *Anti-Semite and Jew* when he "[takes] . . . account of the fact that men must be free to be Jews if that enters into their choice of themselves in the world, precisely without choosing at the same time that all men should be Jews."[29] Caws apparently believes that Sartre's "form of the generalization argument" would commit him to an absurdity inasmuch as it is impossible that everyone be a Jew. Perhaps Caws is just recognizing that those who choose to be Jews would never choose this for all others; if this alternative is pressed, however, it seems to merge into the former alternative, inasmuch as the reason those who choose to be Jews would never choose this for all others is precisely that to be a Jew is to be different from these others—which is to say that it is impossible for everyone to be a Jew.

What makes a Jew different from others who cannot be Jews is similar both to what makes a woman different from those who are not women and to what makes a black man or black woman different from those who are not black. Sex and race are aspects of an individual's facticity. As aspects of the individual's object-side (the way he or she is seen by others), sex and race may, as it were, acquire a superstructure of social interpretation which transforms something close to brute fact into a destiny. What makes sex and race different from Jewishness, according to Sartre, is that in the latter any element approximating brute fact is even more nebulous or possibly nonexistent.[30]

Although women of all races and blacks and Jews of both sexes may have difficulty recognizing themselves in society's views of them as female, black, or Jew, and though they are certainly right to reject society's view of their "destinies," they must nonetheless come to grips with these aspects of their facticity or being-for-others. To deny being a woman, a black, or a Jew would be as self-deceiving as for Sartre's homosexual to deny his past actions. To be authentic, women, blacks, and Jews must in some way choose themselves as women, as blacks, as Jews. Other options are closed to them much as the options of diplomat and sailor are closed to Sartre's waiter and as the possibilities of nonillness are closed to the individual who is ill and who thereby has a diminished "bouquet of possibilities"—"the illness is a *condition* at the interior of which the man is again free and without excuses."[31] Similarly, though, the options of woman, black, and Jew are closed to white, non-Jewish males. The human situation being what it is, for Sartre, "I am perpetually condemned to will that which I have not willed, to no longer will that which I have willed, to reconstruct myself in the unity of a life in the presence of destructions which are inflicted on me from without."[32]

Given Sartre's claims about facticity and being-for-others, it makes no sense to say that one who chooses to be a Jew (or a woman or a black or a diplomat) is thereby choosing that everyone be a Jew (or a woman or a black or a diplomat). Why should Caws or anyone else interpret Sartre's "generalization argument" in this way? Caws seems to be led in this direction by his misreading of Sartre, in particular his assumption that for Sartre there is no human situation (or facticity or being-for-others) independent of particular projects and choices. Thus, contrary to what Sartre says about, for example, having a withered arm or being bourgeois, for Caws, an individual's choices may or may not result in that individual's having a withered arm or being bourgeois. For Sartre, having a withered arm and being bourgeois are aspects of individuals' existences regardless of particular choices they may make. Admittedly the choices are important, since they establish the *significance* of the withered arm and the bourgeois status and determine whether these are handicaps or advantages or irrelevancies. These are choices, however, that simply are not available to those without withered arms and who are not bourgeois. Thus there are for Sartre, as Caws fails to recognize, circumstances sufficiently independent of particular projects that it does make sense for an individual to choose for all those similarly circumstanced—without the additional, question-begging caveat that they must also have projected the same end so that their circumstances can be similar.[33]

Moreover, there seems to be nothing in Sartre's use of the "generalization argument" to keep him from distinguishing types of chosen values. Some values may indeed be moral ones; that is, they may be meant to hold for all human beings. From a moral point of view, any morally permissible choice must be morally permissible for others similarly circumstanced; but it does not follow that every morally permissible choice is a moral choice in the sense that it is meant to hold for all human beings. Within a particular set of circumstances, there may be any number of morally permissible choices. This indeed is the way in which Sartre himself writes when he discusses moral judgments on others. Such judgments are carefully restricted to choices in which individuals try to deny their own freedom or that of others. In her defense of existentialist ethics, Barnes makes a similar point: "The man who values freedom of movement does not insist that everyone must go where he goes. It is the possibility of choice which he holds as the absolute, not the specific choice itself."[34]

To interpret Sartre's moral judgments in this way also avoids a charge Thomas C. Anderson and others have leveled against both Sartre and de Beauvoir: their "willingness to put their lives and honor on the line in support of human dignity seems to bear witness to the very spirit of seriousness they so scornfully reject." Anderson's objection is that Sartre's move from willing one's own freedom to willing that of others involves more than the somewhat Kantian claim "that when I choose a value I, at least implicitly, affirm that all men in a situation similar to mine in all relevant features should also choose this value."[35] As Anderson recognizes, Sartre is claiming more than merely that others should choose in the same way; he is maintaining that others should *be* free.

This move from willing to acting is not, however, the unwarranted move into seriousness that Anderson takes it to be. For Sartre, choosing and acting are not separable. To choose a value is, at least in appropriate circumstances, to act on that choice, and similarly to act is to make value choices, however much we may try to avoid such choosing.[36] Separating choice from action leads to an "abstract morality of good con-science," the "idea that one can be moral without changing the situation" (a morality Sartre clearly rejects in *Cahiers*[37]). Sartre has nothing but disdain for those who, like Garcin in *No Exit*, think they can divorce choice from action: "A man," Garcin declares, "is what he wills to be."[38] Sartre agrees more with Inez's response to Garcin: a man is what he does. Even Garcin is unable to distinguish his intention from his act. He tries to convince himself that he fled his country to further the revolution; yet his death left his action standing alone. He cannot be sure whether his choice was the pragmatic choice of a dedicated revolutionary or the skin-saving choice of a coward.

Neither does Sartre allow action to be divorced from choice. His recognition that man is condemned to freedom is ominous precisely because both action and inaction commit us to value decisions however much we may desire to postpone or avoid such decisions. Sartre's famous example of the woman with her amorous companion makes clear her bad faith as she tries to separate herself from her body in order not to assume responsibility for the acquiescence to which her behavior commits her. As Sartre observes in *Being and Nothingness*, "Our description of freedom, since it does not distinguish between choosing and doing, compels us to abandon at once the distinction between the intention and the act. The intention can no more be separated from the act than thought can be separated from the language which expresses it; and as it happens that our speech informs us of our thought, so our acts will inform us of our intentions."[39] Even words unaccompanied by acts are insufficient: "Commitment is an act, not a word."[40]

Sartre's claim that we must look to acts to inform us of our intentions adds to our previous understanding of why one who attempts to will an end without willing the means is not really willing the end. Many if not all our acts stand in the relation of means to some end or other. Those who profess to will ends while failing, in appropriate circumstances, to do anything necessary to the realization of those ends place themselves in a peculiar position. On the one hand, their actions are condemned as inaction by the ends they purportedly have chosen; on the other hand, to the extent to which intention or choice is inseparable from action, not even the individuals themselves will be able to see connection between the purportedly chosen ends/values and the actions which allegedly embody these ends/values. On the contrary, those actions are likely to be seen, even by the actors themselves, as evidence of choices quite different from those professed. Just as we frequently suspect a Freudian slip when we say the opposite of what we thought we intended, so we generally affirm without hesitation that individuals who never put forth any effort for a cause do not truly want the success they profess to desire.

What distinguishes individuals in bad faith from others is that the former to some extent put themselves beyond the pale of reason, consistency, and truth. They choose not to be bound by reason and truth. Thus they place themselves and their bad faith beyond any reasons which conceivably could count against them. This becomes clearer as we explore, in Chapter 4, the circle of relations with others. Suffice it to say here that Sartre's task cannot properly be understood as requiring him to convince (with reason) those who have placed themselves beyond the pale of reason. All that can legitimately be required of him is that he present reasons that should convince those of us who remain, even with some degree of bad faith, within, as he said in *Cahiers*, "the temporal and the discursive."[41]

If choosing and acting, then, are bound inextricably, Sartre needs little more than universalizability to ground his contention that as moral individuals we must will and further the freedom of all. To will freedom (one's own) as a value is both to will that everyone similarly circumstanced will freedom (his or her own) as a value and *to act accordingly*. If I will that others act in accordance with their choice of freedom as a value, I must at least will that they have the freedom thus to act. Must I not, then, will that they not be oppressed? In addition, how can I be earnest about willing this without working against their oppression?

It is not enough simply to will that I not oppress them. If Sartre is correct in saying that action commits us to value decisions, and vice versa, then my not oppressing them while doing nothing to overthrow the oppression by others compromises my professed willing of freedom for everyone. What I am willing is oppression, as long as I am not personally and actively involved in it. For Sartre, inaction is action; if by action I could prevent some oppression, I am, at least to that extent, actively involved in the oppression. Surely this is the lesson from the Nazi occupation of France that Sartre tries to draw for us in his "The Republic of Silence." Even if my action might not accomplish the overthrow of the oppression, for Sartre, my inaction remains "collaborationist" inasmuch as it makes clear that I find what is going on permissible. If I did not find it permissible, I would be resisting in some fashion or other. In appropriate circumstance, to will is to act.

Although acting may jeopardize the actor's life, the action may follow from an awareness of freedom as the foundation of values, not from the spirit of seriousness which refuses to question the givenness of values. This is just to recognize that freedom is not a contextless will but is embodied and very much dependent on other freedoms, affected by their nonrecognition and vulnerable to their imposition of physical and psychological restraints. As John Stuart Mill so aptly summed up the human condition vis-à-vis others, "a person may possibly not need the benefits of others; but he always needs that they should not do him hurt."[42]

If the claims involved in Sartre's "moral judgment" are indeed analytic, then he avoids the illicit Kantianism of which he so often has been accused. He also avoids a problem arising from an alternative but equally perplexing interpretation. In particular, it might be thought that Sartre, in justifying his "moral judgment," is pointing to the difficulties inherent in the consequences that follow any attempt not to will one's own freedom or to will one's own freedom without willing the freedom of others. Sartre does say that our own freedom "depends entirely upon the freedom of others and that the freedom of others depends upon our own," at least as soon as there is commitment. Certainly it appears to be self-defeating to will one's own freedom "in and through particular circumstances" without willing the freedom of others. Presumably something similar could be said of the attempt not to will one's own freedom "in respect of concrete circumstances."

Whether either of these attempts is in fact self-defeating must be beside the point in terms of moral judgment. To judge actions on the basis of success or

self-defeat is no more open to Sartre than to judge
them on the basis of Kant's categorical imperative,
since Sartre is no more a pragmatist than he is a Kantian. In fact, to base his moral judgment on self-defeat
would leave Sartre in a position similar to that in
which Hume found Wollaston: to say that bad faith is
wrong because it is self-defeating leaves unanswered
the question, What is wrong with self-defeating actions? Whereas lies and self-defeating actions may
seem clearly wrong to most of us, for Sartre simply to
assume that either or both are wrong would be for him
to beg an important question.

Moreover, in the context of Sartrean philosophy, it is
not just that the question What is wrong with self-defeating actions? would be left unanswered. For anyone
familiar with *Being and Nothingness*, a far more significant problem quickly emerges. Sartre is almost no-
torious for having made there such statements as
"man is a useless passion" and "it amounts to the
same thing whether one gets drunk alone or is a leader
of nations."[43] Even if these statements can be interpreted otherwise than at their face value, Sartre simply
has too much to say, there and elsewhere, about the
futility of human actions and too little to say about
their success. When he does talk about something resembling success, it is in terms of failure that somehow succeeds ("loser wins").[44]

Mary Warnock and Wilfred Desan hold bleak views
of Sartre's philosophy. Warnock contends that according to Sartre there is nothing that individuals as individuals can do that will not be futile. Desan presents
the following as the "tragic finale of Sartre's ontology":

> The For-itself is a failure in its inner constitution.
> Being what it is not and not being what it is, it carries
> in itself an insoluble paradox.

The For-itself is a failure in its attitudes toward the other: love, desire, sex are so many illusions. "The hell is other people."

The For-itself is a failure in its conquest of the world: it will never be what it wants to be, the For-itself-in-itself: i.e., God.

"Human being is a useless passion . . . and to intoxicate yourself alone in a bar or to conduct the nations is equally vain."[45]

Although these views are, I think, overly negative in their emphasis on failure, they do point to a problem if self-defeat is to be used as a basis for moral judgment: Sartre just does not seem to allow for the existence of actions that are, in any unqualified sense, successful. His claim that man is the desire to be God, a being haunted by permanency, perfection, and completion, cannot be dismissed simply as a characterization of those in bad faith.

We are left, then, with a position in which futility— the striving for an impossible coincidence with oneself, with one's values, and with others—is far too significant a part of Sartre's thought to allow for any simple, unproblematic condemnation of self-defeat. The analytic interpretation of Sartre's justification of the moral judgment on bad faith allows us to take futility and impossibility as seriously as Sartre seems to have intended them. To condemn bad faith on the basis of a hypothetical imperative that individuals in bad faith themselves in some sense accept, and that commits them to means they refuse to accept, is not to condemn this behavior because it is futile.

Although what I strive for may itself be impossible, perhaps even logically impossible, nonetheless there is an important difference between striving for what is impossible and the logical impossibility of willing the end without willing the means. This difference can be seen in the widely divergent effects of self-awareness in the two cases. In the case of striving for the impossible, self-awareness may have little effect on the project. Just as I can become aware of the futility of such an action as pouring water through a sieve and yet continue my effort, so, it seems, I can become aware of the futility of, for example, my striving for perfection, for coincidence with my values, without this awareness negating my continued effort. As Sartre recognizes, this is not the case with bad faith. As soon as I have become explicitly aware of my attempt to deceive myself, I destroy the project. In his discussion of cynicism in *Being and Nothingness*, Sartre points this out. Unlike bad faith, cynicism, the deliberate attempt to lie to oneself,[46] fails completely; it is ruined "from behind" by the very consciousness of lying to oneself. Bad faith maintains its precarious existence only by avoiding lucidity, by never becoming aware of itself. The logical impossibility of willing the end without willing the means must therefore be distinguished from striving for the impossible. Although the latter requires (and will receive) considerably more development, it at least remains a possibility for the authentic individual even after the former has been soundly condemned by Sartre's moral judgment.

Both the desire to be God and to lie to oneself attempt the impossible; yet they involve the impossible in very different ways. In lying to oneself, one uses the impossibility of what one is doing to justify oneself. To maintain one's project in the face of a dawning recognition of what one is doing, one can buttress one's flagging and threatened belief by noting that every belief is an impossible belief and that one's present freedom-denying belief, in bad faith, thus is justified.[47] Where bad faith requires doing the logically impossible (to will the end without willing the means), striving to be

70

God, to effect a coincidence between oneself and one's values, does not require one to do the logically impossible. The latter requires only that one *strive* for a completion, a coincidence, something one, as a human being, cannot achieve.

Although Sartre proposes that men are free and must create their own values, including their moral values, he develops in his famous "moral judgment" a judgment with which all moral agents can concur whatever the moral values they may have chosen. That is so because this judgment—like the claim that, in choosing values I choose for all people—is analytic: it does no more than make explicit that which is essential to the moral point of view. This is not to say that Sartre tries to base all of morality on such purely formal considerations. Moral values remain to be determined, to be chosen, by each individual. Other moral judgments must be made by each and every moral agent, but moral agents may disagree over these judgments. Unlike the moral judgment for which Sartre argues, these other judgments follow from agents' choices, not from analyses of choice, willing, and the nature of moral values and principles.

While Sartre's moral judgment has nothing to say about what values to choose apart from freedom (which serves as a means to every other valuation), it does enable him to condemn as inauthentic a surprising range of human choices from the relatively innocuous examples of the woman, waiter, and homosexual to the less innocuous "champion of sincerity" to the more vicious Nazis and other racists and oppressive capitalists. This statement may seem especially surprising in view of my claim that Sartre's "moral judgment" is based merely on analytic considerations. That purely analytic considerations can fuel so many condemnations may be taken not as an indication that Sartre has questionably evoked content and concrete values from purely formal and analytic considerations but, rather, as a testimony to the pervasiveness of the human desire to be free without paying the psychological cost, without the burden of the responsibility inevitably conjoined with that freedom. As Sartre, in *Cahiers*, says of the ambiguity of man: "In one sense I am not able to be anything but a man. In another sense: 'It is difficult to be a man.'"[48]

4

Alienation and Individual Authenticity

Heroism is neither an absolute goal
nor a vocation. But if the occasion
calls for it, we'll become heroes if
we've simply learned to do our job
as men, that is, if we are able to
love what we love all the way.
— Sartre, "Julius Fucik"

In *Being and Nothingness*, Sartre gives several examples of individuals who are in bad faith: the woman and her would-be lover, the waiter in the cafe, the homosexual, the champion of sincerity. In addition, in various other works he develops other examples, including that of the anti-Semite and the characters in his play *No Exit*. These individuals in bad faith are, first and foremost, relating to themselves in a particular way; they are denying the ambiguous connection within themselves of being-in-itself and being-for-itself, trying to be an unproblematic identity which they are not and which they cannot be. On the one hand, such an individual may try to deny her or his facticity, her or his situation—birth, education, class or body and its limitations. On the other hand, those in bad faith may attempt to hide from themselves their transcendence, their freedom, their ability to negate, to separate themselves from, to change, alter, or at least reinterpret their situations. Because it is subject to freedom (at least of interpretation), facticity is not regarded by Sartre as unalterable, and this is the sense in which Sartre says one is responsible for a physical handicap, even for one's own birth. The individual in bad faith chooses to hide this recognition from himself or herself.

In bad faith, an individual may reject the ambiguous existence of those who realize they are both being-for-others and being-for-themselves, that they are both being-in-the-midst-of-the-world and being-in-the-world. That is, they may accept one perspective on themselves as "true" while rejecting the other as "appearance," or they may deny that they are both things among other things as well as beings with futures of possibilities toward which they project themselves.

Each is a being-for-others, not just a being-for-oneself. Even if no others are present to see this object-side, nonetheless, each is a being who has been and can be confronted with this aspect of her or his being. The look of another may disclose this object-side, but so may the rustling of a leaf, if the latter is mistakenly taken as a human observer. "Shame" is what Sartre calls the fundamental attitude through which the existence of the other is revealed.

Thus it is not surprising that Sartre's examples frequently involve each of these aspects in a vital way. As individuals try to flee their freedom and responsibility, they may use the fact that they are both being-for-others and being-for-themselves. If they recognize an aspect of themselves in others' looks, they may try to involve those others in the attempt to flee freedom and responsibility.[1]

In the look of the other, there can be a genuine threat, for that look may threaten the fundamental ambiguity which an individual is. To the other, an individual is only his or her facticity, only what the other sees, only a peculiar kind of thing among other things. The other threatens to destroy the ambiguity that one is by turning one into what one is only in part, in the mode of not being it (because one is also transcendence, is also as one sees oneself, and is also one's possibilities and the origin of the sense and meaning of the world).

The look of the other may, however, pose a threat in a different way. To an individual in bad faith, the other may reveal something that is being denied—the individual's object-side. To one who tries to be only freedom, being-for-oneself, and being-in-the-world (as in the examples of the woman in the cafe and the homosexual), the look acknowledges what is denied and thus threatens continuation of this bad faith. To one uncomfortable with her or his own flesh and that of others, as is Lulu in Sartre's story "Intimacy," the touch or look of another from behind is an uncomfortable reminder that one has a back and a behind, a fact Lulu finds especially mortifying.[2]

In addition, to those in bad faith, the look of others may have an appeal. Transcendence, awareness of themselves, and being the cause of the world (its sense and meaning) are the basis of anguish. In anguish, others recognize the extent of their freedom; since they are responsible for their birth, social situation, and bodily handicaps, they recognize that they have no excuse even for these conditions. Terrified by the extent of their freedom and responsibility, they see the look of others as a possible escape. When others look at them and see them only as their facticity, as the way they appear to those others, as things among other things, those in bad faith may be tempted to try to catch on to these "essences" thus bestowed on them. In "Childhood of a Leader," Lucien succumbs to this temptation when he becomes identified as "somebody who can't stand Jews." Basking in his respectability in his own eyes, he concludes: "The real Lucien . . . had to be sought in the eyes of others."3

For those in bad faith, then, the look gives rise to two opposed attitudes toward the other. In one case, the individuals looked at try to reestablish their freedom, which is denied by the other's look. To reestablish their freedom, they look back, thereby turning the other into an object and destroying him or her as a threat. Here, there is a transcendence of the other's transcendence. In the second case, the other is seen as exerting an appeal inasmuch as the look destroys the ambiguity the individual in bad faith desires to escape. Because the other sees this individual as what she or he is (facticity, being-for-others, and being-in-the-midst-of-the-world) and thereby bestows on her or him an essence, the individual in bad faith may try "to incorporate that transcendence within [herself or himself] . . . without removing its character as transcendence."4

Each attempt is a failure but a failure that only serves to motivate the adoption of the other attempt. While admitting failure, Sartre denies any motivated movement beyond these unsuccessful efforts. Consequently, there is a circle of relations with others, at best a negative dialectic—a dialectic in which there is destruction and alienation, but not a dialectic that would involve movement toward overcoming the destruction and alienation. The failure of one attempt can motivate only the adoption of the other; but it cannot motivate a movement beyond both, since, at the heart of each attitude, the other remains present. Thus, since neither can be held separately without contradiction, each remains at the core of the other.5

In such relations with others, for Sartre, there is

failure. However, instead of affirming the possibility of a way out, a success beyond the failure, Sartre proposes that the failure of one attitude leads to the adoption of the other attitude, never to breaking out of the circle. Like Kant's antinomies, both attitudes presuppose an "inadmissible condition."[6] Until this condition is altered, only a circular movement from the one to the other and back again is possible. Sartre's reasons for denying the possibility of a dialectical movement emerge in the course of his detailed analyses of the concrete relations involved in this circle.

In the first attitude toward others—that of love, language, and masochism—individuals try to recover the being that they are for the other. The look of the other both makes them aware of their being-for-others and threatens to alienate from them this aspect of their being.[7] It is as transcendence that each demands the recovery of this being that each is for the other, since, according to Sartre, it is as one responsible for his or her being that the individual lays claim to this being that he or she is. To effect such a recovery, one tries to *absorb* the other, not as an object but precisely as the other-looking-at-one. This requires one to identify oneself totally with being looked at, with being-for-others. Thus the lover tries to "capture" a consciousness, to possess a freedom as freedom.[8]

The failure of this project of love lies in the very alienation of freedom it effects and demands. In demanding to be loved, one admits the alienation of one's freedom from one's existence as being-looked-at. What the lover wants is a similar alienation on the part of the other; yet the other remains transcendent, out of reach, and the effort to capture a consciousness fails. The problem remains even if the individual tries to seduce and fascinate the other.

In seduction, individuals assume their being-for-others; each attempts to fascinate the other.[9] Individuals aim to identify themselves with their object-side and to be recognized as such; but each does so in order to produce love in the other—and once again, there is failure. According to Sartre, one problem is that to love is to wish to be loved. Love thus entails a reference to infinity, which indicates the deception involved in love: to love is to wish to be loved, and to wish for love from the beloved is to wish that the beloved wish that the lover love her or him. Therefore, love is a "game of mirrors." What is posited is an ideal out of reach, something that, for Sartre, accounts for the perpetual dissatisfaction of love. In addition, there is in love a perpetual insecurity, since at any moment the beloved may reestablish his or her transcendence, thus making the lover appear as an object. Finally, the recovery of being which the lover seeks through the beloved can at any moment be jeopardized from without—by others. This, Sartre says, is why lovers seek solitude; even solitude, however, is not sufficient, since, as a being-for-others, the lover exists for all others; thus "love as a fundamental mode of being-for-others holds in its being-for-others the seed of its own destruction."[10]

Love thus proves a failure. Individuals try in love to lose themselves in objectivity, in their being-for-others—but to no avail. Inevitably they are referred back to their own unjustifiable subjectivity, either by their beloveds or by others. As a last resort, they may go the way of masochism; that is, they may try to deny their subjectivity altogether. According to Sartre, this is even more obviously self-defeating, since the harder they try to be mere objects, the more they will be "submerged" by the consciousness of subjectivity. Sartre indicates that it is this very failure that may come to be sought by the masochist.[11]

This failure may become the occasion for one's assuming a second fundamental attitude: indifference, desire, hate, sadism. Rather than identify with being-looked-at, one may posit oneself in one's freedom and try to confront the other's freedom on the ground of one's own freedom. Thus one looks at the other, thereby transcending his or her transcendence. The other thus is turned into an object, since "a look cannot be looked at. As soon as I look in the direction of the look it disappears, and I no longer see anything but eyes."[12]

This indifference (looking back at the other), however, has its difficulties as a response to the other, not the least of which is that one thereby loses any hope of justification through the other. Admittedly, this is a difficulty only for those in bad faith; but for those who seek such justification, this loss of hope is significant. Where individuals once sought through others to acquire an "essence," they now confront the full realization of the fact that they cannot escape their responsibility for making themselves, that they cannot put this off onto anyone else. The individuals are confronted with the terrible necessity of being free, of being condemned to freedom.[13]

Even more important, to look back at the other and thereby turn the other into an object implies that the other's look already has been recognized as a look. Thus there is an uneasiness, which inevitably accompanies even this looking back. So, instead of looking back, one may make oneself desire and aim to possess the other's body to the extent that the other is identified with his or her body. Once again, an impossible goal emerges—namely, that of possessing the transcendence of the other as pure transcendence and at the same time as body.[14]

Desire, therefore, is doomed to fail. It may succumb to a permanent danger that exists for it as an attempt at incarnation. That is, it may, by incarnating itself, lose sight of the incarnation of the other, something it originally sought. Thus the pleasure of caressing may be transformed into the pleasure of being caressed, thereby passing into masochism.[15]

On the other hand, the failure of desire may motivate sadism. Sadism, Sartre says, is also an attempt to incarnate the other; but now it is violence that is used. Through violence, the sadist tries to reveal the flesh hidden beneath the action of the other. Sadism differs from desire; in desire, the for-itself "loses itself in its own flesh in order to reveal to the Other that he too is flesh,"[16] whereas the sadist does not use his or her own flesh but rather instruments in order to reveal by force the other's flesh to the other. Although the sadist attempts not to suppress his or her victim's freedom, but merely to force the victim to identify with the tortured flesh, the sadist, too, is doomed to fail in his or her project. What the sadist wants, in fact, is impossible, since, in spite of the torture, the victim remains the one entirely responsible for having determined the exact moment at which the pain becomes unbearable.[17]

Sadism, like indifference and desire, "bears within itself the cause of its own failure."[18] Sartre proposes two causes for this failure. First, there is the problem that results if the sadist tries in any way to use the achieved incarnation of the other. To apprehend one's body as flesh is to apprehend it in its materiality, as simply being there for nothing. If the sadist achieves the desired goal—the victim's incarnation—then what results is merely a panting body, a flesh the sadist can no longer utilize. As soon as the sadist tries to do so, its absolute contingency is destroyed by being assigned a goal that serves partially to justify it. Thus the sadist confronts an unsatisfactory dilemma: to remain "in a state of contemplative astonishment" before this achieved incarnation, disconcerted because unable to make use of this achievement in any way; or to return to desire, once again becoming troubled.[19]

The sadist, however, is faced with a second difficulty. According to Sartre, this difficulty consists of a new motive harbored by sadism but at a different level. The new motive results from the fact that the sadist actually is seeking to appropriate the transcendent freedom of the victim. Since the victim's freedom cannot be appropriated, such a goal cannot be accomplished; it always remains out of the sadist's reach. Moreover, this freedom escapes the sadist all the more, the more the victim is treated as an instrument. To reestablish her or his own freedom and alienate the sadist, the victim need only look at the torturer.[20] Manifested in the violence of the sadist is the impossible ideal of all violence, recognized by Sartre in *Cahiers*, "that of constraining the freedom of the other to will freely that which I will."[21]

Thus love and desire, both projects in bad faith, are failures. These failures are of greater significance for Sartre than might otherwise be imagined, since, as he tells us, these attitudes are fundamental and are integrated into all attitudes toward the other, the latter being "only enrichments of these two original attitudes (and of a third—hate)."[22] Their failure demonstrates the circle of relations with the other: love fails, and from the death of love, desire arises, only in turn to collapse and give way to love. More generally, all patterns of conduct directed toward the other-as-object involve within themselves, though implicit and veiled, a reference to the other-as-subject, which is their death. As each of these attitudes dies, a new attitude arises, which aims at capturing the other-as subject, which, in turn, dies and gives rise to the opposite conduct.[23]

Why there must be a circle as opposed to a dialectic

in these relations with the other, is seen in the fact that the other is neither only subject nor only object. Thus, according to Sartre, the only consistent attitude toward others would involve their being revealed simultaneously as both subject and object, as both transcendence-transcending and transcendence-transcended; and this, Sartre affirms, is impossible. We may pursue such simultaneous apprehension of their freedom and their objectivity, but this is, for Sartre, an impossible ideal.[24]

Nor, according to Sartre, does hate allow us to break out of this circle. As Sartre sees it, hate is the "final attempt" to escape the circle; it is the attempt of despair. In hate, one acts with full knowledge of the other attempts to relate to the other. In hate, the for-itself seeks the death of the other, thus abandoning its former attempts to become one with the other or to use the other as a means of recovering its own being-in-itself. Now it merely desires to be a freedom without limits, without facticity, without a being-for-others, and thus to do away with its alienation.[25] Hate, however, since it too fails, does not enable us to break out of the circle. Even if hate could succeed in its original project of suppressing other consciousnesses, actually to succeed in its effort to abolish its dimension of alienation, it would have to bring it about that the other had never been—which clearly is impossible.[26]

Even though Sartre notes that after the failure of this final attempt, that of despair, the for-itself has no alternative but once again to enter the circle, to be indefinitely tossed back and forth between these two attitudes, he nevertheless proceeds to add, in a footnote, that the possibility of an ethics of deliverance and salvation is not excluded by these considerations. Such deliverance and salvation "can be achieved only after a radical conversion."[27]

The circle of relations moves between the relations of love and desire, resulting from the fact that both love and desire are attempts to capture the other, who always remains out of reach. As the failure of love is recognized, love collapses and gives way to desire; similarly, desire fails, collapsing and giving way to love. Sartre denies that there can be a dialectic of such relations with others; never can there be a motivated movement beyond the frustrations and failures of each attempt to relate to the other.[28] Like Garcin in *No Exit*, individuals in bad faith will not escape their "hell" even when alternatives are presented and doors are opened to them. They, like Garcin, have committed themselves in a way that requires them to turn once more to their counterparts of Estelle and Inez and the possibilities of relationship represented by those counterparts.

Not even indifference and hate, albeit themselves attempts to go beyond the failures of love and desire, would accomplish such movement, since these too are failures. According to Sartre, the failures of even indifference and hate leave the individual no alternative but to reenter the circle of love and desire. Thus the failure of love eventually motivates only the adoption of desire, and vice versa, and an individual moves around this circle unless and until there occurs a "radical conversion" from the bad faith of these attempts.

In affirming a circle of relations with others, Sartre does not thereby indicate, as many of his interpreters believe, that all human relations "are bound to be hopeless struggles in which neither side can be satisfied."[29] Commenting on *No Exit*, Sartre says, " 'Hell is other people' has always been misunderstood. People thought that what I meant by it is that our relations with others are always rotten or illicit. But I mean something entirely different. I mean that if our relations with others are twisted or corrupted, then others have to be hell. . . . Fundamentally, others are what is most important in us for our understanding of ourselves."[30]

Thus Sartre does not condemn all human relations to the hell depicted in *No Exit* and presented (more theoretically) in *Being and Nothingness*; rather, he makes a philosophical move which requires that the only way out of this circle is radical conversion. Sartre's analyses indicate not only that individuals caught in this circle will not and cannot be motivated by the failures and frustrations of their various attempts to relate to others but also that these individuals will be impervious to any reasons that could count against what they are seeking. Because they seek what they may even recognize as impossible, neither will they be motivated by their failures and frustrations to escape from the circle, nor can their failures and frustrations count for them as reasons against what they are doing. Simply put, there is no possible motivation for a movement beyond these frustrating relations with the other.

Thus, in this somewhat limited way, Sartre denies a dialectic in relations with others and affirms instead a circle of such relations. The alienation introduced by the look remains and is not overcome as the individual is tossed from one attitude to the other. There may be enrichment of one attempt by the other *within* the circle but no motivated movement *beyond* the circle. Unfulfillment of attempts to relate to the other does not, and cannot, point outside this circle to that which would fulfill, since the demand for fulfillment involved here is a demand for that which cannot be.

What is involved in these relations with others is a demand for the simultaneous apprehension of the other's freedom and objectivity. This is a demand for that which cannot be, since, to become aware of the other as an object is to destroy by one's very look the freedom of which one had hoped simultaneously to become aware. Sartre's analyses indicate that those caught in the circle of relations are faced with a dilemma: try to become aware of the other's freedom and subjectivity as object (indifference, sadism, hate), or try to become aware of the other's objectivity as freedom (love, language, masochism). Either awareness has built in its own undoing, since the other's freedom and objectivity are not subsumable under one another. Because, in an unconverted individual's awareness of the other, the latter moves between the two poles of subjectivity and objectivity, the former has no alternative in the face of the defeat of one way of relating to the other but to adopt the other way.

By affirming a circle in these particular relations with the other, Sartre does not necessarily reject the possibility of a dialectic; rather, he rejects only the possibility of a dialectical advance out of the circle of relations. What he rejects is a dialectical advance in a situation where the demand for fulfillment, which should provide the impetus for going beyond present nonfulfillments, is itself a demand for what cannot be. What Sartre rejects becomes clearer if his circle is contrasted with the dialectic evident in Hegel's account of the master-slave relationship.

In his *Phenomenology of Mind*, Hegel presents the failure inherent in the master's desire for recognition. Whereas both the master and the slave desire recognition from the other, there is a marked contrast between the failure of the master's desire and the slave's dialectical success. According to Hegel, the master's desire for recognition from the slave is a desire for what cannot be attained. Insofar as recognition requires a certain reciprocity—a mutual recognition of each by the other—the master's striving to be recognized is at an impasse.[31] The slave's recognition that the master is master will hardly count as the recognition sought, inasmuch as the master does not deign to recognize the slave as much more than a thing, an almost inhuman consciousness. In Sartre's terms, the master demands something much like recognition of his[32] being-as-subject from a being that he has turned into nothing but a being-as-object, and such a recognition simply cannot be; only a subject can recognize another subject. The master seeks recognition he cannot obtain from a slave.[33]

On the other hand, according to Hegel, the slave, by being a slave, may actually attain the satisfaction of his original desire for recognition. At the outset, the slave fights with the master for this recognition but eventually acknowledges the importance to himself of his own life. Thus he surrenders, thereby making the other a master and himself a slave. The slave is then relegated to a dependent status in being defined by the master as a thing. Although it looks as though the slave would thereby have lost the opportunity to satisfy his desire for recognition, according to Hegel this is not so. On the contrary, as the slave develops himself in his role as slave, an alteration occurs that parallels the defeat of the master in his role as master. As the slave works, he imposes himself on the things he toils on, thereby confronting himself with his own image objectified in the world. By seeing and coming to recognize himself, he achieves the self-recognition the master vainly strives to achieve. In this alteration, the slave's bondage passes into its opposite: "real and true independence."[34]

Thus there is on the part of the master a breakdown, or failure, within the role itself: eventually the master's striving to be recognized proves unsuccessful. The recognition as master he thought he had attained through the slave's recognition of him turns out not to be the recognition he desired; for him, the slave's recognition cannot truly count as recognition. Nor can he move beyond this failure, since his desire to be recognized as a master is itself a desire that will not allow him to surpass or overcome such failure. He is at an impasse.[35] Although Sartre is correct when he later observes that history indicates most masters also worked and were recognized by other masters,[36] this observation does not affect the inevitability of the failure of the master's desire vis-à-vis the slave.

Surpassing or overcoming is possible only for the slave. The slave begins with lack of recognition and dissatisfaction with the conditions of his servitude. This dissatisfaction, according to Hegel, allows the slave to overcome the failure of servitude and satisfy his desire for recognition. The slave's desire for recognition is not satisfied by his present condition of servitude; at the same time, his desire differs from that of the master. Unlike the master's desire, the slave's desire for recognition is not, by its own demands, condemned to failure.

Like Hegel, Sartre claims that certain relations with others are governed by a demand, or desire, that is doomed to fail by virtue of the very nature of what is demanded.[37] In both love and desire, one wants what cannot be attained: assimilation or negation of the freedom of the other. Thus the relations Sartre describes are similar to the desire of Hegel's master: all involve a desire for what is impossible. All lead to an impasse—in Hegel, a dialectical dead end, in Sartre, a circle.

It is because all participants in the relations of love, language, masochism, indifference, desire, hate, and sadism are in positions similar to that of Hegel's master that Sartre can "subjectivize"[38] the master-slave section of Hegel's *Phenomenology.* In other words, no one in the circle of relations resembles Hegel's slave. Those in the circle of relations desire what is impossible and, therefore, desire what work could in no way help them attain. This clarifies a point made by Iris Murdoch, who notes that Sartre has indeed left out references to work—"the pointer toward liberation" in Hegel. What remains is that "Sartre's lovers are engaged in perpetual speculation about the attitude of the other. The project is appropriative, their torment a torment of the imagination. . . . There is no suggestion in Sartre's account that love is connected with action and day to day living; that it is other than a battle between two hypnotists in a closed room."[39] Like Hegel, Sartre is aware of the importance of work; in *Cahiers* he observes that the "true relation to others is never direct: [but rather] through the mediation of work."[40]

Inasmuch as individuals in bad faith, apart from their relations with others, have been seen to desire a similar impossibility with respect to themselves—to be an identity of facticity and transcendence, being-for-others and being-for-itself, being-in-the-midst-of-the-world and being-in-the-world—they can also be likened to Hegel's master. Alisdair MacIntyre makes a similar point, but uses a different part of Hegel's *Phenomenology* to do so, when he compares the individual in bad faith who desires to be For-itself-In-itself with Hegel's unhappy consciousness. MacIntyre notes that these individuals can be compared only if Hegel's unhappy consciousness is "lifted outside the dialectic of history."[41] Sartre acknowledges this when he describes "human reality" (presumably in bad faith) as an "unhappy consciousness with no possibility of surpassing its unhappy state."[42] Those caught in Sartre's circle of relations are "outside the dialectic of history" precisely because the demand they make is a demand for what is impossible, and thus, like the demand of the master, a demand that prevents a dialectical movement of overcoming, of surpassing the failure in the direction of its satisfaction.[43]

Given the impossible demand made by such individuals in bad faith, we can understand why Sartre speaks of "deliverance" and "salvation" from this circle, and why he says such deliverance and salvation must be effected by a "radical conversion."[44] The undialectical notions of "deliverance," "salvation," and "conversion" are underscored by de Beauvoir in her discussion of conversion. She notes that human beings make themselves a lack, but that they can deny this lack as lack, thus assuming their failure. This assuming of failure, however, is contrasted with Hegelian acts of surpassing; the assuming of failure is, rather, she affirms, a matter of conversion.[45] Norman N. Greene expresses the same point in a slightly different way when he notes that with respect to Sartre's radical conversion the abandonment of the original project of bad faith could not be motivated since what counts as a reason or a motivation is determined by the original project itself.[46]

Thus, in bad faith there is a circle or a self-enclosure. All evaluations are made within the original bad-faith determination of what is to be valued. Lack of success in realizing one's values can count against a particular attempt to realize these values but not against the values themselves. From the failure of one attempt, the individual in bad faith can only move to another, and, when that attempt fails, try again.

A similar circularity or self-enclosure holds for choices and projects in general. The value of all particular choices and projects is established within an original determination of value R. M. Hare recognizes a similar point in distinguishing between decisions of principle and justifications of individual moral judgments. He notes that some moral judgments are "verified by reference to a standard or set of principles which we have by our own decision accepted and made our own."[47] The standard or set of principles used in this verification cannot, in turn, always be justified or verified by reference to another standard or set of principles. Hare avoids an infinite regress by recognizing that there are basic moral principles we decide to accept by making a "decision of principle," which can be justified only by "complete specification of the way of life of which it is a part." Such a decision of principle is not unfounded or arbitrary, since, as Hare sees it, "it would be based upon a consideration of everything upon which it could possibly be founded."[48] At the same time, Hare recognizes, such a decision of principle is not justified in the more normal sense, since there are no more basic moral principles by reference to which it could be verified. Sartre made the same point in *Cahiers*, where he refused to say that we are "unjustified," noting that such a claim would require "a system of justification in which we would not find our proper place."[49] Consequently, he argues, we are neither justifiable nor unjustifiable.

Hare recognizes—as does Sartre—that, in a sense, nothing can count for or against one's ultimate commitments or decisions with respect to moral principles and values. On the basis of these, one supports or rejects other choices; but the ultimate decisions with respect to principles and values cannot themselves be similarly supported or rejected. They determine what is to count for and against other choices; there are, and can be, no more ultimate decisions that determine what is to count for and against these ultimate decisions. This means that Hare's decisions of principle and Sartre's original or fundamental project are, apart from questions concerning their internal self-consistency, invulnerable to attack. Other than such internal inconsistencies, there is nothing that can count for or against them—except from the point of view of *another* decision of principle or fundamental project.

Individuals in bad faith deal with the impossibility of what they try to accomplish—willing the end without willing the means—by reconciling themselves never to being satisfied. Thus they reconcile themselves to irrationality and thereby protect themselves from problems that would arise for them from their internal inconsistencies. Certainly they will not be bothered by their failures, especially inasmuch as these failures themselves are what such individuals eventually come to seek. What they seek may indeed be impossible, but that only means impossibility is not, after all, such a bad thing. They seek the impossible and choose not to be rational, not to be moral, not to restrict themselves in any way to what is within the limits of probability. Their failure, however constant, cannot count against what they seek, nor can it motivate them to seek something else. By their striving, they keep themselves in the circle Sartre describes. Like Hegel's master, they are, dialectically speaking, at an impasse.

Individuals relating in bad faith to themselves and to others cannot, then, be looked to for any sort of negative evaluation of their present situation. Because they desire what cannot be, they experience failure; yet their failure can only logically count against a particular means chosen to realize their desire; it does not and cannot count against their desire itself. From the point of view of those with such desires, any negative evaluation of the desires themselves must seem arbitrary.

Hegel's master-slave dialectic can be pressed further to indicate that any overcoming, as well as any negative evaluations of the master's predicament, can emerge only from the slave. The slave desires what is possible, and this desire allows the slave to move beyond, to overcome or resolve, the failures and antinomies of the master-slave relationship. Besides being an impetus to such overcoming, the desire allows the slave to evaluate negatively the master's position. From the perspective of the slave's desire and of failure overcome, the master's situation will seem pathetic, inferior, wrong. Dialectically, a higher perspective is established by virtue of the slave's desire, a perspective from which negative evaluations of the master's situation can be made nonarbitrarily and without begging the question. This is so because the master and the slave, at least in part, want the same thing: recognition. The slave achieves recognition, though not the recognition-as-master sought by the master. As the slave moves history on, the master remains caught by virtue of his desire in a situation where, at least vis-à-vis the slave, no recognition that can count as recognition can be achieved.

In *Saint Genet*, Sartre presents an individual—Jean Genet—with a desire more closely resembling that of Hegel's slave. Genet's desire differs radically from that of bad faith, and Genet succeeds in a way those in bad faith do not and cannot. Genet's desire differs from the desire to be God as this is depicted in *Being and Nothingness*; thus it indicates that the latter was indeed, as Sartre later described it, an analysis of one ontological level, namely that of bad faith, or, as he says in *Cahiers*, "an ontology before conversion."[50]

As Sartre observes in *Cahiers*, the "pursuit of Being is hell."[51] For one with a desire such as Genet's, the failure that makes this pursuit such a hell may lead to conversion, while others simply may deny it in bad faith. It is important to see that the "hell" of bad faith motivates a conversion only for individuals with a certain kind of desire. No doubt, it is because of this connection with conversion that some have seen in *Saint Genet* the work on ethics promised by Sartre at the end of *Being and Nothingness*.[52]

In *Saint Genet*, Sartre again refers to failures and to circles, but here he refers to triumphs as well, speaking of evil as a "pure contradiction" that "destroys itself" and of a "dialectical progression which . . . deviates into a circular movement" in which Genet "can keep his balance only by moving faster and faster." In addition, however, Sartre claims that Genet's endeavor to be evil ends in failure which also is a triumph inasmuch as Genet "is playing loser wins" and since the "impossibility of evil *is* the greatest evil."[53]

Unlike the failure in *Being and Nothingness*, Genet's failure is one that involves him in a dialectical movement or progression. Genet's dialectic can be seen in Sartre's summary of Genet's life:

> One must will an act to the very end. But the act is alive, it changes. The goal one sets at the beginning is abstract and consequently false. Little by little it is enriched by the means employed to attain it, and ultimately the concrete goal, the true goal, is what one wants at the finish. . . . In willing himself, unreservedly, to be a thief, Genet sinks into the dream to the point of madness, he becomes a poet;[54] in willing poetry unto the final triumph of the word, he becomes a man; and the man has become the truth of the poet as the poet was the truth of the thief.[55]

A parallel with Hegelian dialectic (surely a conscious one) is obvious here. The goal set at the beginning is abstract and false; it is enriched and gradually changed through the means employed to attain it. Finally, Genet's goal at the "finish" is a "concrete" and "true" goal, his attainment being the truth of the earlier stages. In mentioning the "possibility of a dialectic," de Beauvoir notes that "Sartre has given us a precise example in *Saint Genet*."[56]

For Sartre, this affirmation of a dialectic in the life of Genet involves recognition of another fundamental desire rather than a new analysis to replace his earlier analyses of bad faith and inauthentic relations with others. Unlike the self-deception of bad faith, Genet's is a "profound will . . . which assumes the impossibility of evil." Genet, therefore, confronts and assumes the impossibility where those in bad faith only recognize peripherally the impossibility of their projects as they utilize this impossibility in order to disguise their projects from themselves. Genet is also realistic; Sartre tells us: "When a realistic will applies itself unremittingly to its object and when it finds itself, without having been diverted by an external influence, in the process of willing the opposite of what it wills, there is a fundamental contradiction in its project."[57] When Genet discovers a contradiction in what he wills, he confronts it rather than trying to avoid, defuse, or obscure it, as do those in bad faith. For example, when Genet realizes that he wants both being and nonbeing, that he wants both to accept the world and to reject it, and that he cannot both accept and reject the world except in a dream, he becomes an actor and turns to the imaginary. To refuse the world is to modify it through work, to "accept many things in order to modify a few."[58] For Genet, however, even though the world is unacceptable, he is unable to change it; thus his rejection can be only a gesture. Being realistic, though, he manages to turn that gesture into an act and to turn himself from an actor into an agent—by writing.[59] Through his fiction Genet tries to triumph over those who had seen him as a thief; as a writer, he "will plunge his hands into their souls, he will knead that white dough and will give it the shape he wants it to have. The consciousness of others is the medium in which man can and must become what he is."[60]

Genet wins. He does triumph:

> He comes and goes. He is free. It is almost eight years since he was last in prison. He has money, "honorable friends." This common-law criminal lives part of the time in Paris and part in Cannes, leading the life of a well-to-do bourgeois. He is "received." He is taken up by the followers of fashion, is admired by others, but as he has not stopped associating with burglars and queers, he goes from drawing rooms to Montmartre bars, plays *The Mysteries of Paris* all by himself, and, because he comes from nowhere, feels at home everywhere.[61]

Genet also has lost, however: "When Genet put out his hand to sweep the board, the stake had disappeared."[62] He had tried to get society to accept him as he was, as an evildoer, to accept him at the same time that it rejected him. Instead, society honors him for his talent. Moreover, those who honor him have themselves been changed by his writing; they either become the tolerant Genet detests and has denounced, or they reveal themselves as not of a piece. That is, because Genet's writings disturb them, they show themselves as less than just. Because of this transformation, Genet fails to receive the recognition he sought from "the Just." Furthermore, Genet himself has changed. He is not the thief he tried to get the Just to accept: "He discovers *himself* among men, not as *the* Thief nor *the* Saint, but as a certain man who is like everybody and nobody."[63] Genet thus illustrates a point Sartre makes in *Cahiers*: "all triumph is a reversal. I no longer recognize my end, that is to say that I no longer recognize myself, I am prey for others, obliged to suffer consequences that I have not willed, facing a reality which, through its materiality, necessarily degrades my project; destined by myself, enemy to myself, I have made a fall into the world."[64]

Thus he fails. He even loses the "need, desire and occasion to write." Yet he wins, not only his physical freedom but a freedom from phantoms by which he had been haunted. He discovers people in general "are neither just nor unjust but, at one and the same time, just in the depths of their injustice and unjust at the very source of their good will."[65] He has played the game of loser wins and become a human being.

Although, for Sartre, there is no historical progress that leaves behind those in bad faith, impotent in their bad faith, nonetheless, there are significant similarities between Genet and Hegel's slave and between those in bad faith and Hegel's master. Like the slave, Genet succeeds, although Genet's success seems considerably more problematic. Both those in bad faith and Hegel's master are caught up in desiring in such a way as to deny themselves the possibility of any success whatsoever. Both place themselves in a position where their failure cannot count against their desire, nor for them will the success of others count in favor of the desire of the latter and against their own desire. Yet neither are their respective failures and successes totally irrelevant. Just as the slave and the master desire the same thing, albeit in different ways, so Genet and those in bad faith desire the same thing in different ways. However much they differ in the *way* in which they desire what they desire, and however much this difference enters into and transforms what they desire, *to the extent* that there is a commonality in what they desire, their respective successes and failures are relevant and do count for the parties involved and for those of us who to some extent stand outside the options we more or less dispassionately survey. In the final analysis, however, this commonality will not lead all of us to the same conclusion, most especially not to the same way of pursuing our own desire. As Sartre observes at various points in his career, for each of us "the chips are down." If, for example, I have chosen the failures and irrationality of bad faith, I have chosen to pursue the desire to be God in such a way that the failures—my own or those of others in bad faith—cannot count against my desire *as modified, as pursued.*

Sartre gives other examples of "loser wins"; the most familiar are from a short story and several of his plays. In "The Wall," Pablo Ibbieta, awaiting death before a firing squad, experiences the disintegration of the revolutionary's world in which he had lived. Freed from the seriousness of his past and its values, which no longer matter to him now that his illusion of immortality has been shattered, Pablo decides to play a trick on his captors, who have promised his release in return for information concerning the whereabouts of another anarchist, Ramon Gris. Pablo must choose between his own life and that of Gris. Although he realizes that Gris' life has no more value than his own, he nonetheless chooses, with a "droll sort of gaiety," to send his captors on a wild-goose chase through a cemetery rather than to the farmhouse where he believes Gris is hiding.[66]

Still awaiting his death upon their return, he enjoys imagining the ludicrousness of the serious but entirely futile search of the cemetery by his captors. When they return and free him, Pablo is bewildered; later he learns that Gris was captured in the cemetery. At this point, Pablo bursts into hysterical laughter. Loser wins, although the last laugh is on himself. He is freed from the certainty of immediate death, but he is also freed from a final vestige of seriousness. His laughter is evidence of his lucidity as he now recognizes that even his playful choice of his own death failed as a result of the fact that the consequences he anticipated depended on others over whom he had (and continues to have) no control.

In Sartre's play *The Devil and the Good Lord*, Goetz, concluding that it is relatively easy to do evil, resolves to do good. In spite of his resolution and his valiantly persistent effort to accomplish his goal, Goetz has nothing but evil to show for his perseverance when his actions and their consequences are weighed a year later. As he murders the priest to whom he was to prove that it is possible to do good, Goetz declares: "The comedy of Good has ended with a murder." He now realizes that he must begin with the crimes and hates of those he is trying to help: "I must demand my share of their crimes if I want to have my share of their love and virtue. I wanted pure love: ridiculous nonsense. To love anyone is to hate the same enemy; therefore I will adopt your hates. I wanted to do Good: foolishness. On this earth at present Good and Evil are inseparable. I agree to be bad in order to become good."[67]

Though the play ends at this point and we remain ignorant of the ultimate outcome, Goetz is now playing loser wins. He feels assured of victory if his men are more afraid of him than they are of the enemy. To bring about the "kingdom of man," Goetz says, "I shall make them hate me, because I know of no other way of loving them. I shall give them orders, since I know of no other way of obeying. I shall remain alone with this empty sky over my head, since I have no other way of being among men. There is a war to fight, and I will fight it."[68]

This character, de Beauvoir tells us, is made to do what Sartre himself was unable to do. Goetz becomes the "perfect embodiment of the man of action as Sartre conceived him" by accepting the "discipline of the Peasant War without denying his own subjectivity, within the enterprise he preserves the negative moment."[69] As Sartre says, "Goetz, in the final tableau, accepts the relative and limited ethics which is proper to human destiny: he puts history in place of the absolute."[70]

With Jean Aguerra, in Sartre's scenario *In the Mesh*, winning through failure is more evident. Although aware that his deportations and other acts of "tyranny" will result in his overthrow and execution, Aguerra knows that he has avoided war long enough to save the revolution. He will be cursed, but he knows he has done what he could to bring about justice.

In the play *Dirty Hands*, Hoederer, like Aguerra, also exemplifies Sartre's game of Loser Wins. Hoederer admits that his hands have been plunged in filth and blood. He argues, against the idealistic and principled Hugo, that for one who loves people and wants to change the world, "all means are good when they are effective." Even though Hoederer is killed, he wins in several ways. First, he is vindicated in his analysis of Hugo as an intellectual and not a true revolutionary ("just good enough to make an assassin"). More important, though, Hoederer, though he dies, triumphs: his policies win out, while Hugo finally sees his own act of murdering Hoederer as at best a "farce."[71]

What these literary and real-life examples have in common is, first of all, their lucidity; each is clear about what he is doing or attempting to do in a way that those in bad faith are not and cannot be. There is within each, though perhaps in different degrees, a reliance on himself, on that which is within the limits of his probabilities. Each confronts failure. Even Goetz is likely to be killed by his men or, at best, to reach a recognition such as that of Genet: that he and others are neither good nor evil but rather both, that the world will remain as it was, with good and evil inseparable.

Alienation, then, is inevitable. History may or may not vindicate, as it happens to vindicate Hoederer. Even if it does, it will do so in at best an ambiguous way. Like Genet, an individual may attain the recognition sought, but at that point he will find that everyone has changed; those from whom recognition was sought are different, and so is the seeker. Individuals will fail to coincide with their goals, with themselves, and with others with whom they may try to involve themselves. They and others remain free and therefore are never identical with their projects, with what they are, or with each other, whatever their relationship. They remain what they are not, their facticities, their being-for-others, their being-in-the-midst-of-the-world. The look of another can always confront them with an aspect of themselves over which the other seems to exert more control than they themselves exert.

Although alienation is inevitable, there is an alienation that can be avoided or overcome. It is with respect to this avoidable alienation that the game of loser wins must be understood. In winning, authentic individuals avoid or overcome the sort of alienation inflicted on themselves by those in bad faith. Those in bad faith are at odds with themselves in a way that an authentic individual is not: they cannot allow themselves to see clearly what they are doing or the kind of being they are. In their attempts to deceive themselves, they alienate themselves from what they are and from what they are doing in a way that the authentic individual does not.

In addition, the authentic individual may win by

overcoming, as did Genet, the alienation imposed by others. Genet had been seen as a thief by "the Just." Like the Jew Sartre describes in *Anti-Semite and Jew*, Genet had a necessity imposed upon him, that "of assuming a phantom personality, at once strange and familiar, that haunts him and which is nothing but himself—himself as others see him." Sartre could say that Genet thereby is "over-determined" just as he says this of the Jew: "But the Jew has a personality like the rest of us, and on top of that he is Jewish."[72]

It is the society of "the Just" and of anti-Semites that imposes such additional determinations on Genet and Jews. The resulting alienation is avoidable. If Genet and Jews respond in bad faith to these gratuitous object-sides of their existence, that is, if they try to be either just a thief or just a Jew, or to deny being a thief or a Jew, theirs is a secondary bad faith, since it is possible only because of the previous bad faith of "the Just" and of anti-Semites. This may be why, when Sartre writes of the inauthentic Jew, he quickly adds, "the term 'inauthentic' implying no moral blame, of course."[73] Given the situation in which they have been placed by society, however, authentic Jews must affirm themselves as Jews and demand their rights as Jews *and* as human beings.[74]

The ambiguity of the Jew in an anti-Semitic society parallels somewhat and is illuminated by that of the slave discussed in *Cahiers*. Sartre recognizes that the slave's willing himself as "underman," as nonessential to the world of the master, subjectively involves mystification and bad faith and objectively is "pure complicity with the master." Nevertheless, Sartre notes the ambiguity in this resignation, since, against the morality of force, the slave's freely willing his own "under-humanity" is at least "an effort to regrasp in freedom the radical negation of all freedom . . . [in

101

which the slave] seeks to affirm man."[75] The ambiguity of the slave's resignation, like that of the Jew's complete identification with or complete rejection of his Jewishness, leads Sartre to be much less judgmental in his analysis of the bad faith involved.

For Sartre, the Jew is largely if not wholly the creation of the anti-Semites and in times of calm is denied even the opportunity to regain his freedom by revolting against his oppressors: "[when] all is calm, against whom is he to revolt? He accepts the society around him, he joins the game and he conforms to all the ceremonies, dancing with the others the dance of respectability."[76] Unlike Genet, the Jew may encounter no particular resistance. Unlike Genet, the Jew may be free but is nonetheless robbed of her or his successes; these successes are mysteriously devalued, because they are, after all, the successes of a Jew.[77] A Jew may choose authenticity, but this, as Sartre notes, "in no way [serves] as a solution on the social and political level: the situation of the Jew is such that everything he does turns against him."[78]

Thus there exists a kind of alienation imposed by some societies, which authentic individuals cannot always overcome. Although this alienation is not inevitable, overcoming it requires fundamental changes in society.[79] On the other hand, some forms of alienation are overcome or avoided by the authentic individual. Self-alienation, in particular, is avoidable; it is particularly in this way that authentic individuals "win." They lose in that they are beings for whom alienation of a certain sort is inevitable: they cannot coincide with themselves, with their values, and with others. Yet they "win," since, by accepting their freedom and the limitations of the human condition, their own in particular, they overcome the alienation of bad faith and may even overcome, as does Genet, an alienation imposed on them by society. Thus, as Sartre so movingly says of Genet, "he becomes a man."

Without illusions, knowing that nothing can save or justify him, Sartre himself reaches a similar point at the end of his autobiography, *The Words.* "If I relegate impossible Salvation to the proproom, what remains? A whole man, composed of all men and as good as all of them and no better than any."[80] Such a person no longer seeks salvation through writing; rather, that person can respond with appreciation, as did Sartre, when, for example, a sympathetic critic such as Jeanson analyzes the ethical implications of Sartre's thought and gives him, as Sartre says, "an image of myself which is sufficiently close for me to recognize myself, yet sufficiently alien for me to be able to assess myself."[81]

5

Play versus Seriousness

> Every human reality is a passion in that it projects losing itself so as to found being and by the same stroke to constitute the In-itself which escapes contingency by being its own foundation, the *Ens causa sui*, which religions call God. Thus the passion of man is the reverse of that of Christ, for man loses himself as man in order that God may be born. But the idea of God is contradictory and we lose ourselves in vain. Man is a useless passion.
> —Sartre, *Being and Nothingness*

In Chapter 3, we saw how Sartre is able to make a moral judgment condemning bad faith while at the same time affirming that each person must choose his or her own values. The latter affirmation is not as unproblematic as it might be, however. First, it has been argued that the relativism inherent in this claim is untenable, either because it renders action impossible or because it leads to logical absurdity. Second, Sartre's emphasis on the futility of all human actions further complicates his claims about values and their creation. In this chapter I shall develop play as Sartre's way of resolving both problems, that of relativism and that of futility.

Søren Kierkegaard suggests one problem with rela-

tivism in ethics when he proposes that individuals become "hypothetical" if they attempt to create their
own values *ex nihilo* apart from any foundation in
what they are and their dependence on God.[1] If values
depend on our choice, and if we become aware of this
dependence, we must also recognize that the continuation or endurance of all values similarly depends
on our choice. We remain free to alter or tear down
whatever values we have chosen. We become hypothetical because values depend on our choosing and re-
choosing. If all values are in some sense on a par, there
is nothing but our choice to determine our selection of
and adherence to one value rather than another. Moreover, this choice must continually be repeated before
anyone can act—with the result that the choosing individual will be like Zeno's runner dividing the stadium to infinity but never completing the course.
Unable to extricate himself from this infinite regress
of choice, Kierkegaard's hypothetical man, like Dostoevsky's underground man, is plagued by inertia, the
inertia of indecision. Like Buridan's ass or John Barth's
Jacob Horner,[2] such individuals simply are unable to
act.

In *The Concept of Morals*, W. T. Stace develops a different problem, one which he believes confronts the
ethical relativist on the psychological rather than the
logical level. Stace objects that, if the ethical relativist
is correct, moral judgments on other cultures and
other individuals are at best expressions of the "vanity
and egotism of those who pass them."[3] His objection
may not trouble an ethical relativist inasmuch as it
presumes an objective basis for moral judgments,
something the ethical relativist denies. It thereby begs
the question, simply failing to recognize that the very
affirmation of moral values and principles requires
that, implicitly or explicitly, they be affirmed as hold-

ing for everyone, at least for those in similar circumstances.

Stace protests that it is difficult for individuals to adhere to moral standards that are *ex hypothesi* no better than any others.[4] This criticism is more problematic, especially in the context of Sartre's philosophy. Can individuals become aware of their freedom and of the fact that they choose values without at the same time recognizing that at each and every moment they remain free to maintain in existence or to abolish previously chosen values? Is Stace correct in his fear that the recognition that values are arbitrary and unjustifiable must render difficult or highly unlikely any individual's continued adherence to particularly demanding moralities? How can individuals not be demoralized? How can they continue in enterprises where the stakes seem so high but where there can be no justifications of their choices of values? Even such a sympathetic critic as Anderson affirms that Sartre's and de Beauvoir's "willingness to put their lives and honor on the line in support of human dignity seems to bear witness to the very spirit of seriousness they so scornfully reject."[5]

Finally, there is the problem with futility. In *Being and Nothingness*, Sartre recognizes what he considers the failure of all human projects. Man is a "useless passion"—the desire to be in-itself-for-itself—that is, God—an impossible being. Insofar as all actions sacrifice man to this impossible goal, and all are doomed to fail, they are equivalent. Thus, "it amounts to the same thing whether one gets drunk alone or is a leader of nations." Admittedly, Sartre follows this recognition by questioning whether freedom must "necessarily be defined in relation to a transcendent value which haunts it."[6] Anderson pursues this suggestion, proposing that human beings need not always take this unattainable goal as their primary goal. Instead, he maintains, Sartre's answer to this problem of futility is that, realizing the vanity of one's goal of being God, one can "neglect" this goal and take some other end—for example, freedom—as one's primary goal. If individuals were to choose freedom as their ultimate value, they would "work to remove restrictions to choice and to the attainment of goals sought."[7] Although Sartre often refers to the desire to be God as an original, or fundamental, "choice," Anderson's suggestion has to do with choice of a different sort—with reflective choice, choice as it is ordinarily understood.

Anderson's answer to this problem seems to be on the right track. Sartre does indicate that we always will be haunted by the desire to be God. At the same time, he proposes that a radical conversion from bad faith is possible and he develops examples of individuals like Genet whose actions are not merely futile. Moreover, according to Sartre's *Critique of Dialectical Reason*, societies may overcome scarcity and oppression even though they too are "haunted" by an impossible ideal of society as an organism.

Against Anderson's solution to this problem stands the fact that individuals like Genet do not simply "neglect" their impossible goals and turn to possible ones, futility being thereby abolished; rather, Genet pursued his impossible goal in a determined, clearheaded, earnest way until he managed to succeed even though he failed. Through his writing, Genet tried to get others to accept him as a thief. He "won" insofar as he secured his release from prison, had "honorable friends," was "received," recognized, and admired. He failed, however, inasmuch as his writing transformed both himself and "the Just" to whom it was addressed. Where "the Just" were disturbed by his writing, they showed themselves as less than just. Through his writing, Genet too was changed by his discovery of himself as a man among men, "like everybody and nobody" but no longer the thief he had tried to get "the Just" to accept.[8]

Neither are impossible goals neglected and futility overcome by Sartre's Marxism in his *Critique of Dialectical Reason*. In the *Critique*, Sartre details attempts—by aggregations ranging from groups to institutions—to surpass the separated, unreciprocal existence of individuals; he calls this "seriality." For Sartre, each attempt to create the group as a unity involves contradictions, with the result that eventually there will be a lapse back into seriality. The group's activity has limits; although it is formed in opposition to alienation, its activity always embodies itself and thereby alienates itself in matter, and this activity is the source of the group's undoing.[9] Although notable achievements may be made during this development from the group to the institution, for Sartre there is nonetheless an ultimate futility with respect to the attempt to achieve a community.

The futility recognized in the *Critique* can be specified more precisely by noting that the group exists between the seriality of the collective and the unity of the organism. The idea of the practical organism becomes for the group an "Idea" in the Kantian sense: "an unrealisable task which becomes regulatory by constantly positing itself as capable of being realized the next day."[10] The group is thus haunted by an impossible ideal just as, according to *Being and Nothingness*, the individual is haunted by the in-itself and by the impossible desire to be God. For the group as for the individual, the unity sought cannot be attained.

Futility also plays a significant role in Sartre's novels, plays, and short stories. Often, however, it is juxtaposed to the theme of "loser wins." Individuals in Sartre's fiction are, like Sisyphus, involved in enterprises in which they cannot succeed, at least not in an unqualified way.

Finally, in *Cahiers* Sartre observes explicitly that the "authentic individual cannot through conversion suppress his pursuit of Being because there would be nothing else [*car il n'y aurait plus rien*]." For this reason, Sartre concludes that the authentic individual will always have a "poetic side" inasmuch as poetry is invoked (or lived) by those who are able, with or without a conversion, to love being lost, to love failure.[11]

If all actions are recognized as futile, failing to achieve what is sought, how can we continue to pursue goals we realize canot be accomplished? Like Stace's problem with relativism, the problem with futility is a psychological one. It looks as though the authentic individual depicted by Sartre would be demoralized. As attempts to realize impossible goals, all actions are equivalent. By recognizing the ultimate futility of human action, Sartre places all human beings in the frustrating position of Sisyphus. We are haunted by *value*, by the desire to be God, by the need to achieve community; yet inevitably our efforts fail as we try to coincide with our values, with ourselves and with others. Because of the kind of being we are, an unbridgable gap remains. The problem of futility is how to live with this realization.

In his ethics, Kant encountered a lesser problem with futility. For him, morality demands a perfection we cannot achieve; all we can do is continually strive for it. Convinced that *ought* implies *can*—and aware that, insofar as morality involves action, it demands a continual striving to achieve perfection—Kant proposed that immortality and the existence of God are necessary postulates of morality. We must postulate both an infinite progress toward perfection and the existence of God who would see this process as complete in an eternal now and who would reward us with happiness in exact correlation with our worthiness of it. Otherwise, we would find ourselves in a psychologically problematic position, with the demands of morality practically impossible, "strained to an unattainable destination."[12]

For Sartre, there is no God, nor can there be one. God is a logical impossibility. Moreover, even if there were a God, this would not help resolve the problem with futility that Sartre faces. No god could offer an escape from Sartre's problem of futility, inasmuch as Sartre's problem is based on an impossibility that differs from Kant's merely practical impossibility of human perfection. For Sartre, what we are makes it impossible for us to coincide with ourselves, with our ideals, or with our fellow human beings. Postulating an infinite struggle and a God to see this struggle as completed cannot resolve this problem. If a human being is a vain, useless passion to do and be that which is rendered impossible by virtue of her or his being human, then God's eternal vision would be of no more use than is human temporal vision in envisioning this goal as accomplished.

Thus, a Sartrean ethics must resolve more than merely the psychological problem of inevitable failure to achieve perfection. It must present a viable way of living with the realization that ultimately one's actions are futile precisely because the achievement of one's goals requires that one be a radically different kind of being than one is. Moreover, such an ethics must provide an answer to Kierkegaard's logical problem with chosen values and to Stace's more psychologically oriented challenge to an ethics based on such values. What Sartre says about "play" provides the resolution to all three problems.

Both commentators and critics have noted the necessity and significance of play. William Leon McBride, for example, links play and futility: "if we take seriously the inevitability of the gap between the individual's projects and their accomplishment, which is itself the result of the gap that Sartre has discerned between being-in-itself and being-for-itself, *all* labor must have about it something of the futility, the nonseriousness, that we have described as the essential characteristic of play."[13] Similarly, Douglas Kirsner recognizes the "ontological necessity" of play for the Sartrean individual who is eternally absent from himself or herself: "Man is doomed to never cease playing roles for he can never take on an authentic identity: he is condemned to be free."[14] And Ralph Netzky, writing in *Philosophy Today* a decade ago, acknowledges the importance of the opposition between play and the spirit of seriousness.[15]

Sartre himself contrasts play with the "spirit of seriousness" in which the "serious man" tries to give "to himself the type of existence of the rock, the consistency, the inertia, the opacity of being-in-the-midst-of-the-world." One who is serious, Sartre says, is concerned with consequences: "at bottom [he] is hiding from himself the consciousness of his freedom; he is in *bad faith* and his bad faith aims at presenting himself to his own eyes as a consequence; everything is a consequence for him, and there is never any beginning. That is why he is so concerned with the consequences of his acts."[16] Play is concerned with consequences as well, but in a very different way. The serious person sees consequences as beyond her or his control; indeed, such an individual sees herself or himself as a consequence of other causes. In play, on the other hand, consequences are viewed as the result of free activity. As Sartre says,

What is play indeed if not an activity of which man is
the first origin, for which man himself sets the rules,
and which has no consequences except according to
the rules posited? As soon as a man apprehends himself
as free and wishes to use his freedom, a freedom, by the
way, which could just as well be his anguish, then his
activity is play. The first principle of play is man himself; through it he escapes his natural nature; he himself sets the value and rules which he has established
and defined.[17]

That play is vital to ethics is indicated by the way in
which Sartre characterizes it as a "particular type of
project which has freedom for its foundation and its
goal" and, more explicitly, by what immediately follows this characterization of play in *Being and
Nothingness*:

It is radically different from all others in that it aims at
a radically different type of being. It would be necessary to explain in full detail its relations with the
project of being-God, which has appeared to us as a
deep-seated structure of human reality. But such a
study can not be made here; it belongs rather to an *Ethics* and it supposes that there has been a preliminary
definition of nature and the role of purifying reflection
(our descriptions have aimed only at *accessory* reflection); it supposes in addition taking a position which
can be *moral* only in the face of values which haunt the
For-itself.[18]

In *Cahiers*, Sartre presents play as a break from the
spirit of seriousness, as, we should be able to conclude,
vitally connected with authenticity:

Risk: I don't prove my freedom only by the pure subordination of the exterior world; I prove it also in agree-

ing to struggle against it. . . . At the same time, the challenge is *play*: it is a rapture with spirit of seriousness, expenditure, annihilation, passage to the festive side. The festival in effect is liberation from the spirit of seriousness, the expenditure of economics, the ruin of hierarchy, and the absorption of the other by the Same [*le Meme*], of the objective by intersubjectivity, of order by disorder. Thus the *apocalypse* will be one of the extreme types of human relations.[19]

On the basis of these statements about play, we can construct resolutions to the problems of relativism and futility with which this chapter began. Sartre denies any preexisting justifications for our action, recognizing that even God could not bridge the gap between our goals and our accomplishments. Sartre affirms that we must create and sustain in existence our own values as exemplified in our choices and actions.

In play, we create without any preexisting values. Children at play create characters, dialogues, situations, and actions—even values that may differ from those taught by their parents. Adults invent games and sustain them in existence, for example, by freely following the rules they have created, thus "*playing* the game." Sartre's authentic individuals must create their own values through their actions; moreover, they must recognize that their choice of these values is not a necessary one and is not supported or justified by anything whatsoever. Like one who invents a game, those who are authentic know they could have chosen differently; but, like the creator of the game, they did not in fact choose differently. They chose—which is not to say that their decisions are irrevocable; they remain free to revoke the chosen value as a value but not to abolish the fact of their having chosen this value.

Whereas both the creator of the game and the authentic individual remain free to alter or reject their game and chosen value, respectively, both individuals may proceed to act in accordance with their choices without undertaking an infinite number of reaffirmations. To decide to act and then to act does not require an infinite series of decisions in each of which one's previous decision is affirmed, any more than the runner of Zeno's famous race is required to complete an infinite number of movements before he can reach the end of the stadium.

In his novel *Nausea* and in the three-volume *Roads to Freedom*, Sartre develops such characters as Roquentin and Mathieu, who have difficulty acting and who afflict themselves with paralysis. They are "serious," however. They seek justification or are unable to accept responsibility for their freedom and its consequences. They are not authentic; they do not play.

For there to be an unbridgeable gap between decision and action requires, first of all, that there be a gap between decision and action. For Sartre, this is simply not the case. Anderson and others fail to recognize that, for Sartre, choosing and acting are not so easily separable. To choose a value is to act, in appropriate circumstances, on that choice; similarly, to act is to make value choices. If Sartre is correct, one can avoid neither choice nor action. Not to choose is itself a choice, and, generally, not to act is itself an action. To assume that one can choose without acting or act without choosing, or avoid both choosing and acting, is to assume a position foreign to Sartre's. Thus, if the hypothetical person's problem is a problem of ever *beginning* to act, then it is a problem that never arises in a Sartrean framework.

The hypothetical person's difficulty, however, can be interpreted in such a way that it is not resolvable by Sartre's recognition that to choose is to act, and vice versa, and that both action and choice are unavoidable.

114

These recognitions fail to provide an answer to the question, Why should one continue to reaffirm a past choice by undertaking step by step each action in the chain of actions that may be necessary to complete a project or to finish a game? This interpretation of the hypothetical man's problem more closely resembles Stace's psychological problem of sustaining previously chosen values than it does Zeno's paradox.

If the problem is that of sustaining one's commitment, particularly to demanding values, in the face of the realization that one's chosen values have no external, objective justification, here too play points the way to a resolution. Although this may be a more empirical and less properly philosophical problem, at least an analogy with other forms of play suggests that the psychological problem may not be as serious as Stace believes. Individuals have developed and participated in games that demand extraordinary preparation, skill, and exertion; surely some of these individuals were aware that there were other, less demanding possibilities no more (and, of course, no less) objectively warranted or justified. This suggests that Stace and others who agree with him are merely begging the question in favor of absolutism. Otherwise, surely they could ask, "Why would an individual continue to adhere to demanding standards?" and be willing to entertain as a perfectly acceptable, sufficient answer: "Because he or she chooses to do so." Authentic individuals must acknowledge that they are free not only with respect to the world and the values of others but with respect to their own past choices. They must realize that they and they alone bring into existence and sustain in existence the values on which they act.

The very question, Why would an individual continue to affirm previously chosen values? either ignores the fact that any other values would be equally arbitrary, or it assumes that we are free to cease choosing and acting. We may choose to end a game or discontinue a project. We may even do so for what we consider good and compelling reasons. If, however, we recognize that there are no such reasons for continuing the game or the project on which we have been working, surely this, in itself, is insufficient reason to drop it. To play this objectivist game of demanding good and compelling reason, and to do so even-handedly, requires that there be sufficient reason for whatever we do—even if we discontinue the project. Too many of Sartre's critics fail to recognize that for every Why? there is a Why not? that is just as difficult to answer. Many a project may be completed for no better reason than that it was initiated. Such seems to be the point of the "dilemma of Morality" in *Cahiers*:

> If the goal is *already* given, it becomes a fact and derived from being, not a value; but if the goal *is not* given, then it is gratuitous, . . . the result of caprice. This is what has been badly understood: the goal must be willed in order to be; here is the first characteristic. There is a goal only for a freedom which wills itself free. But, on the other hand, the existence itself of man as free and transcendent project poses necessarily the question of the goal in this sense that it puts the universe in question in its being. . . . There is here the original emerging not of goals, but of questions. The answers are not given. . . . [I]t is necessary not to *find* them but to invent them and will them.[20]

Does this invalidate commitment, as some of Sartre's critics have affirmed? Because Merleau-Ponty's criticisms of Sartre have been so influential, let us consider his claim, "From the single fact that it is a question of committing *oneself*, that the prisoner is also his own jailer, it is clear that one will never have other bonds than those one currently gives oneself and that one never *will* be committed."[21] In one sense Merleau-Ponty is correct: one is never bound by what one has chosen or done. One can always free oneself from the direction specified by past choices and actions. To the extent Merleau-Ponty is correct, what he says is not very interesting. It becomes a significant objection to the possibility of commitment only when it is conjoined with his view of Sartrean freedom as the "pure power of doing or not doing, a power that fragments freedom into so many instants, . . . the freedom to judge, which even slaves in chains have."[22] Yet this is a view of freedom Sartre, in his 1946 essay "Materialism and Revolution," quite rightly rejected as a "pure idealistic hoax."[23]

If we take into account what Sartre, even in his early work, said about facticity, being-one's-past, and being-for-others, Merleau-Ponty's objection seems to reflect more his misunderstanding of Sartre than the impossibility of commitment in Sartre's view. Although one may choose to fight the privileges or dispossessions of class, to ignore hunger or other bodily appetites, to take stands on injustices previously ignored, to quit playing the buffoon for others, there remain throughout this choosing aspects of existence that cannot be abolished and which to some degree set the parameters of present choices. Moreover, as Jeanson points out, reflective choice always takes place against a "background of unreflective life," which provides motivations for particular choices and renders the will intelligible to itself.[24]

Although it is important to acknowledge my freedom with respect to my facticity, past, and appearance for others, to do so requires more than Merleau-Ponty's "magical fiat" to act on this freedom. I may choose no longer to acknowledge a particular motivation as relevant to my present choice; but as long as I remain within the "ensemble of projects that I am, . . . my fundamental choice of myself," I at most only modify secondary projects.[25] Given the ambiguous relation of my transcendence and my freedom, my being-for-myself and my being-for-others, my being my past and my not being my past, I never can become an absolute subject (Merleau-Ponty's view of Sartre notwithstanding); I cannot simply examine, at each and every moment, a past commitment afresh and, as it were, with no strings attached. Even the spontaneous upsurge of unreflective freedom, the source of fundamental choice of self, always is related ambiguously to facticity, the past, and being-for-others. Although this unreflective level of freedom keeps one from being bound within one's fundamental choice of oneself, at the same time it will not be easy to disengage oneself from that fundamental choice, for, after all, it delimits all those things that can count as good reasons for an alternative choice. Any deliberate effort to change one's motivation and thereby effect a conversion will be "abortive" as long as it involves "impure or accessory reflection"—a reflection operating *within* the fundamental choice—since "impure reflection is an abortive effort on the part of the for-itself to be *another* while *remaining* itself." "Pure reflection, the simple presence of the reflective for-itself to the for-itself reflected-on" is necessary for the radical conversion vital to morality; such reflection "must be won by a sort of katharsis."[26] Such conversion seems hard won, not accomplished by "magical fiat."

What Sartre says in *Cahiers* supports Jeanson's claims. There, Sartre explicitly rejects both a transcendently based morality and a purely subjective one. He cuts a middle ground between these, maintaining that to reject the transcendent-object approach to values

118

does not lessen their bindingness on us.[27] In the same volume he amplifies on this middle ground in rejecting the alleged implication that the For-itself's choice is capricious: "This doesn't mean at all, quite to the contrary, that the For-Itself ought to choose to define itself by the caprice of the instant (because caprice of the instant is caprice only in appearance; it takes its shape as caprice from a foundation of constant choices). . . . That which will define its love is the concrete sacrifice that it makes today and not what it intends or what it feels."[28]

Finally, and most explicitly, *Cahiers* reaffirms Jeanson's interpretation by containing the observation that choice is always in the context of an already constituted personality and thus is not capricious: "But if man qualifies himself by his choice, caprice no longer has meaning because, insofar as it is produced by a personality already constituted and which is 'in the world' [*au monde*], it inserts itself at the interior of a choice of itself and of an already existing Good. It is the instantaneous attention at the instant. But in order for there to be attention at the instant, it requires a duration that temporalizes itself, that is to say, an original choice of Good and of me in the face of Good."[29]

From Sartre's analysis of freedom and reflection, I conclude that commitment is meaningful at each of two levels. First, as we have seen, fundamental choice of self to a considerable extent binds my future choices. If this choice is one that values freedom, it requires an ensemble of projects and motivations that will call for actions in support of freedom. Thus one is committed to such actions. Second, some of these called-for actions may themselves be (or involve) additional secondary commitments whereby one deliberately tries to bind future decisions by making conflicting decisions as difficult as possible. This level of commitment is paralleled in Sartre's later writing by what the group does in its attempt to restrict or bind in advance, by promises and by terror, the freedom of its members.

The problem of futility is, I believe, a more difficult one, which more centrally involves play. Play enables the authentic individual to overcome the problem of futility. A player in a game participates *as if* the rules or values of the game have some sort of necessary, objective reality and validity. At the same time, as long as players are playing and not so caught up in winning that they mistake the game for something else, they recognize that these rules and values have no such necessity or objectivity. In other words, one who plays avoids the seriousness of those who no longer play. In avoiding this seriousness, such an individual also avoids the serious person's reaction to futility. Even inescapable futility is not an insurmountable problem for those who play. In play, we may exert great effort to balance unbalancable objects and to fill sieves with water.

Does it make sense, however, to place life and honor on the line, as did Sartre and de Beauvoir? Did they, as Anderson claims, thereby slip into the spirit of seriousness? Although people frequently risk their lives in games, we tend to view play as a frivolous activity, to assume that those who risk their lives in play are doing so not for the game but for some reward external to the game itself. With such reasoning, *we* move into seriousness and thus beg a fundamental question by assuming that there *are* ready-made values, some of which may warrant the risking of life and some of which clearly do not. More fundamentally, we beg the question Sartre deals with by assuming that life *is* valuable, that only something objectively higher in value could possibly warrant an action that risks life.

If Sartre is correct, *we* determine the extent to which our lives are valuable, as well as their value vis-à-vis other values. The values created and sustained in play are not frivolous in comparison with those of the players' lives; values have no existence apart from individual choices. Certainly there is no hierarchy of values independent of such choices. Serious human beings try to convince themselves otherwise, but their consternation over the irrationality of those who play "for keeps" cannot count as a legitimate objection to the unserious play of those who are authentic.

In using play to resolve the problem of futility, Sartre provides an answer that is reminiscent of Kierkegaard's response to the futility affirmed by the clergyman: "A man can do absolutely nothing himself." Although the clergyman's claim renders futile all action, and though it would seem to justify our doing anything whatsoever (or nothing at all), Kierkegaard argues that this need not be the case:

> But if a man proposes to himself every day to bear in mind and existentially to hold fast what the clergyman says on Sunday, understanding this as the earnestness of life, and therewith again understanding all his ability and inability as a jest: does this mean that he will undertake nothing at all, because everything is empty and vain? Ah, no, for then precisely he will have no occasion to appreciate the jest, since the contradiction will not arise which brings it into juxtaposition with the earnestness of life: there is no contradiction involved in that everything is vanity in the eyes of a creature of vanity. Sloth, inactivity, the affectation of superiority over against the finite—this is poor jesting, or rather it is no jest at all. But to shorten one's hours of sleep and to buy up each waking period of the day and not to spare oneself, and then to understand that the whole is a jest: aye, that is earnestness.[30]

For Kierkegaard—or, at least, for one at the lower level of the religious state, "Religiousness A,"—humor and the comic cancel the contradiction experienced by those who realize that "against God we are always in the wrong."[31] The "law of the comical" is, Kierkegaard says, "quite simple: it exists wherever there is a contradiction, and where the contradiction is painless because it is viewed as cancelled." The contradiction experienced by the ethical/religious person at this level can be canceled by a "legitimate comic apprehension."[32]

The interesting thing about play as a resolution to the problem of futility is that it changes both the nature and the outcome of the project. Genet confronted the impossibility of achieving what he sought. He recognized the contradiction in what he willed— that he wanted both to accept and to reject the world— and that he could do what he willed only in a dream. He thus turned to the imaginary, to gestures—to writing fiction. Genet did not "neglect" his impossible goal; rather, it continued to guide his action, although he no longer sought it in the same way.

Instead of Anderson's neglect of the desire to be God, a reflective transformation of this goal seems to be in keeping with these later developments in Sartre's philosophy. In bad faith the desire to be God is taken as a goal; if recognized as an impossibility, it becomes an excuse justifying all failure, including the failure of bad faith itself. Although the authentic individual and the group do not necessarily neglect impossible goals, they do pursue such goals in radically different ways. To some extent they turn from impossible goals as such to what is within their control. They thereby exist, as Sartre recognized in an early work, in "despair"—the sense that we must "limit ourselves to a reliance upon that which is within our wills, or within the sum of the probabilities which render our action feasible . . . that we should act without hope."[33] In an interview with Benny Levy (also known as Pierre Victor), Sartre (then seventy-five) continued to affirm: "Despair was the belief that my fundamental goals could not be achieved, and that, as a consequence, human reality entailed essential failure."[34] Two years earlier in comparing Levy to himself, Sartre admitted to de Beauvoir that he, like Levy, wanted everything: "Of course you don't attain everything, but you must want everything."[35]

This does not mean that impossible goals must be neglected; rather, it means that, in authenticity, they become regulative.[36] They must be interpreted in such a way that they can guide behavior without requiring the presumption that such things are or can be. Here, Kant's famous phrase *as if* is relevant. Although individuals and groups may be unable ever to achieve the harmony and unity represented by such ideals as God and organism, the ideals nonetheless may guide behavior. Concretely, this would mean that, instead of trying to be, for example, an identity of being-for-others and being-for-self, individuals would strive to be (for themselves) what they appear and to appear to be what they are (to themselves). The authentic individual would assume responsibility for and attempt to harmonize as far as possible those disparate aspects of herself or himself where the individual in bad faith tries to unify, to reduce them without remainder to one another, and, failing to unify, then uses the impossibility of such unity as a justification for any and all behavior.

It is important to note that regulative ideas had been discussed fairly extensively though never published by Sartre in *Cahiers*. There he speaks of "two antinomous requirements, both of which must be conserved":

"The first is to define *with the oppressed* a positive Good in the light of which Evil appears as evil and which is necessarily hypostatized as a goal in the Future. This is the *directive maxim of action*, the regulative idea. . . . The second is *not to take as serious* this infinite Idea, because it remains suspended in the freedom of men to come, and that it is not able to be for them an absolute End that we should have inscribed by our actions in things but only a proposal. We have to *impose* our Good on our contemporaries, to *propose* it to our descendants. Thus, it is a relative-absolute, like ourselves."[37]

The problem is, on the one hand, if one aims at the city of ends and if this goal is ideal, then, as Sartre says, "hope disappears." On the other hand, if the end is projected into some far-off or impossible future, then the end remains beyond and outside the means and potentially able to justify any and all means. It would then lead to "the maxim of violence": "the end justifies the means." In addition, as we have seen, the impossibility of the goal may play an important role in the self-justification of bad faith. In fact, Sartre tells us in *Cahiers*, violence is in bad faith, since it is Manicheistic, believing "in an order of the world given but disguised by evil wills" and since it pushes destruction while counting "on the riches of the world to support it and perpetually furnish new things to destroy." The connection between bad faith and violence goes even deeper, inasmuch as the lie, so central to the understanding of bad faith, always is made in the name of freedom, and "happens as if one said: 'If you freely will to attain this end, you ought to will the means of attaining it, therefore you ought to will to be lied to [or any other means—the maxim of violence] if it is necessary.'"[38]

To avoid defeatism, violence, and bad faith, Sartre proposes that the goal must be viewed not "as being by

relation to the means in the exteriority of indifference
. . . [but rather] as the organic unity of the means." In
other words, such a goal is not "the last link in the
causal series A, B, C, D, E, F . . . but . . . is the organic
totality of the operation." Because Sartre's resolution
of his antinomy requires that we see the end *in* the
means, and not as totally separate from them, the
means will truly be a "prefiguration of a city of ends":
"The solution of the antinomy is to not distinguish the
end from the means and to treat man as end in the
same measure in which I consider him as means, that
is to say, to cause him to think himself and to will himself freely as means in the moment to the extent to
which I treat him as end and making it known to him
that he is absolute end in the decision itself through
which he treats himself as means."[39]

Later, in *Cahiers*, Sartre states this antinomy and its
resolution somewhat differently: "As soon as a goal is
assigned to the human species and as soon as this goal
is finite, as soon as one envisions it as a reality, . . . the
species becomes an ant. The given closes again on itself. It is necessary that the goal be infinite. But if it is
beyond attainment for each generation, this is dis-
heartening. It is necessary that it be finite. This means
that each accomplish it and that it is then to be accomplished later. A finite enterprise for everyone in the
context of the infinite enterprise of humanity."[40]

Realizing the nonidentity of facticity and transcendence, and the inescapability of both, authentic individuals would affirm themselves as both, thereby
seeing their facticity as subject to their freedom and
their freedom as inevitably situated in their facticity.
Thus they harmonize and coordinate these aspects of
themselves to the extent such aspects can be harmo-
nized and coordinated. Sartre can then say, as he did in
his interview with Levy, that "human reality entailed

essential failure" vis-à-vis one's fundamental goals and that nevertheless the despair that acknowledges this essential failure is not the opposite of hope, as it appeared to be in Sartre's earlier characterization of despair. Hope, rather, is an "essential element of an action" inasmuch as "I cannot undertake an action without expecting that I am going to complete it."[41] This apparent reinstatement of hope makes sense only if fundamental goals are taken as regulative. For the authentic individual, the regulative ideal of unity or coincidence will act only as a lure, as a perpetual challenge and constant source of dissatisfaction, without, however, being taken either as realized or as realizable—without, that is, being taken as a concrete aim.

Lest we think this emphasis on hope reflects a serious turn away from Sartre's earlier thought, it is important to note that Sartre, in *Cahiers*, cautioned that if "the objective situation renders a structural ensemble of projects and enterprises impossible and anachronistic, . . . our enterprise will become a fictive reality, . . . a *played* enterprise." This must be avoided, Sartre says, "since we know that it is impossible for us to take the poetic and tragic attitude of preferring failure, and we will continue to play out the impossible so that our conduct itself might be a demand, a claim." Sartre's conclusion even then was that morality and the tactic of freedom imply "that one should never shut oneself up in an enterprise, never allow one to flow like water in a well but always be able to struggle against it."[42]

Although we continue to "play" the impossible, these goals should be taken as regulative, and the concrete aims that we form in their light must take into account circumstances and probabilities. Sartre seemed to be referring to such concrete goals earlier in *Cahiers*, where, in discussing with approval the analytic significance of Kant's "You ought, therefore you can," Sartre observes: "Only it is not at all to restrict itself to the intention. It is necessary that it achieve itself in the act. It is not a matter only of conceiving and willing an act; it is also necessary that the situation make it possible and that I know this."[43]

Authentic individuals, as Sartre says in the interview with Levy, "no longer want to be God, . . . no longer want to be *causa sui*."[44] As soon as these goals become regulative, a reorientation is effected: emphasis is placed on freedom and what is within the limits of probability for the particular individual. In a sense, the authentic freedom does turn "its back upon this value [of *being* God, or *causa sui*]." It puts "an end to the reign of this value."[45] The goal of *being* has been replaced by one of *striving*. As soon as the impossible goal becomes regulative, it guides the authentic individual's striving for harmony and condemns the non-regulative goal of simple identity.

Where authenticity resembles ordinary play is in the fact that in both we accept this lack of coincidence between the apparent and the real. In ordinary play, we may recognize this and nonetheless continue to play and enjoy the game. Authentic individuals must act in a similar manner. With the latter, however, the emphasis is not on enjoyment but on lucidity, on the awareness that they are doing what they can as free, responsible human beings.

However much authentic behavior involves play, it involves something more, and this additional element is important to Sartre. In his view, not just any game will do. The waiter in the cafe, the well-known example from *Being and Nothingness*, may be playing at being a waiter; but for Sartre, this game is unacceptable.[46] In his desire to be God, the waiter tries to achieve the ultimate identity of facticity and freedom through a game of pretense, of self-deception, which ignores and attempts to deny altogether the ambiguity of his own existence as an uneasy tension between necessity and freedom, the determinateness of the past and the openness of the future, and the inevitably disparate ways in which he is seen by others and by himself. As Netzky observes, rather than conclude " 'that the waiter is *only* playing,' we might lament the fact that he is '*only* serious.' "[47]

In such bad faith, individuals try to achieve their ultimate goal through magic and incantations much like one who, in fear, magically causes by fainting the "disappearance" of the threat.[48] By fainting, the fearful person relinquishes or denies responsibility for the body and its actions and retreats into pure subjectivity. Futility enters into the fainter's behavior but in a way entirely different from the way it did in the foregoing discussion of the problem of futility. There is no *problem* of recognizing one's intentions in the consequences of fainting. As we know, fainting does not remove the threat; rather, it leaves the one who faints vulnerable, unable to resist or escape from the threat. The consequences here may be the opposite of the safety and security sought. The waiter seems to be in a similar position, inasmuch as his robot-like behavior is and will remain antithetical to what he sought: the more he becomes object-like, the *less* he is the subjectivity-as-object he sought to become. The opposition between the goals and the actual consequences of actions makes apparent the moral problem with bad faith discussed in Chapter 3, namely, that those in bad faith try to will the end without willing the means. In this sense, consequences can count *against* an individual's actions and choices although, given the ultimate futility of human actions, consequences can never *justify* the value of any other actions and choices.

What this analysis of consequences means, then, is that Sartre can affirm a particular way of playing as that appropriate to the authentic individual. Joseph P. Fell refers to this, aptly I think, as "lucid play."[49] Such individuals accept and affirm the futility of their efforts to actualize their ultimate goal; yet they continue to do what they can to accomplish it. In *Iron in the Soul*, for example, Mathieu recognizes the futility of his action and impending death—that ambushing those particular Nazi soldiers will "merely put their time-table out by ten minutes!"[50]

Men like Hoederer *(Dirty Hands)* and Genet *(Saint Genet)* acknowledge and accept their freedom and the ultimate futility of their actions, yet enter the fray, resolved to control and change what they can. Although they may neither control nor change the course of history, nevertheless they act. They realize their finitude and essential ambiguity and work within these even while striving toward an impossible goal. Mathieu sums up this attitude as he indicts himself and a cohort for their previous political noninvolvement. Implicitly recognizing that their participation in politics might not have prevented the present confrontation, he still affirms: "At least you would have done all you could."[51] As Sartre says in *Cahiers*: "The historical agent ought to accept that his work prolongs itself only by proposition and that the spirit which animates it will continue to act only in the manner of a residue. But at the same time, *he ought to take all precautions* to retard as long as possible the moment of alienation."[52]

6

Alienation and Society

> Thus, we must at the same time
> teach one group that the reign of
> ends cannot be realized without
> revolution and the other group that
> revolution is conceivable only if it
> prepares the reign of ends. It is this
> perpetual tension—if we can keep it
> up—which will realize the unity of
> our public. In short, we must
> militate, in our writings, in favor of
> the freedom of the person *and* the
> socialist revolution. It has often
> been claimed that they are not
> reconcilable. It is our job to show
> tirelessly that they imply each other.
> —Sartre, *What Is Literature?*

Existentialists frequently are criticized by Marxists for alleged acquiescence to the status quo of capitalist society. Marxists see in various existentialists' affirmation of an insurmountable otherness, an inescapable alienation, little more than a "crude apology for the capitalistically alienated social relations of production."[1] Like other existentialists singled out in this attack, Sartre writes of the inevitable alienation confronted by individuals, of insurmountable objectification, of unavoidable futility in human enterprises. Is his attack on existing social structures and institutions, then, nothing more than "an absurd, irra-

tionalistic, empty 'ought'"— "an idealistic mystification which condemns all attempts directed at a
practical transcendence of alienation to the fate of a
Quixotic enterprise"?[2]

If Sartre had begun and ended his analysis of society
and alienation with his account in *Being and
Nothingness* of the us-object and the we-subject, this
accusation would have been a difficult one against
which to defend him. In *Being and Nothingness*, following his discussion of the circle of concrete relations
with others, Sartre recognizes and discusses the possibility of certain concrete experiences of community.
He describes two such experiences, that of the "us-object" and that of he "we-subject." Both seem to offer a
temporary psychological respite from the circle of relations with others. In both experiences the encounter
with the other is complicated by the appearance of a
third party. Whereas before this arrival there were just
the two individuals looking at each other—being
tossed from the attitude of love, language, and masochism to that of indifference, desire, hate, and sadism, and back again—now a third party arrives and
looks at both. In experiencing himself or herself as
being looked at, each of the original parties experiences the possibilities of loving and desiring the other
as objectified and turned into dead possibilities.[3] Thus
the appearance and look of the third party reduce to
the same level the two originally opposed situations.
There is no longer any priority for either, since, as far
as the third is concerned, both sets of possibilities are
equally dead possibilities. The earlier conflict is transcended by the third party and becomes in her or his
look a "factual given which defines . . . and holds . . .
together" the other two. The other two experience a
solidarity with one another, since each experiences in
shame a being-outside in which they are organized into

an objective whole and no longer are fundamentally distinct. In this way they experience themselves as an us-object.[4]

The we-subject may result from their response to the shame of being an us-object. In fact, Sartre says, there are two ways they may respond to their shame. On the one hand, each may assert his or her individual claims to selfness by looking in turn at the third party. Even though the threat embodied by the third was experienced as a threat to *them*, they each in turn look at the third party and thereby seem simply to move back into the circle of relations with others, in effect, merely changing partners. On the other hand, they may transform themselves into a we-subject, by for example, undertaking some common action against the intruder.

The we-subject can arise in other ways. With or without a third party appearing on the scene, the original parties may become constituted as a "we" by virtue of finding themselves both looking at something else. Sartre illustrates this with the scene in front of a cafe where, observing the other patrons and being observed by them, an individual is in a situation of conflict: each is a being-as-an-object for the other. Suddenly, as an incident occurs in the street, the individual becomes, along with the others, a spectator of this event and experiences herself or himself nonpositionally as being engaged in a "we."[5] This feeling oneself in the midst of others as a "we" may also be experienced when one is engaged with others in a common project. This is possible, however, only if the individual has already accepted a common end and common instruments, and has rejected any personal ends that go beyond the collective ends presently being pursued.[6]

Sartre makes it clear that the "we" cannot arise from an experience of the world as an instrumental complex. In opposition to the position taken by Martin Heidegger, Sartre maintains that if one is to experience oneself and others as undifferentiated members of the "we" to which manufactured objects refer, the other must already be given in some way. Opposing Heidegger's primacy of the world of "the they" *(das Man)*— the world of "no one," since all are so well blended into the instrumental complex as to be inconspicuous and indefinite[7]—Sartre argues that a person "who had not already experienced the Other would in no way be able to distinguish the manufactured object from the pure materiality of a thing which has not been worked on. Even if he were to utilize it according to the method foreseen by the manufacturer, he would be re-inventing this method and thus realize the free appropriation of a natural thing."[8]

If the "we" were merely a derivative experience in the sense of presupposing a prior experience of the other, it might offer a serious, viable alternative to the two fundamental attitudes toward others that result in the frustrating circle of relations. Even though we might see something like the circle of individual relations reproduced at the group or communal level, still, the "we" could offer a way of relating to others that is radically different from those developed in the circle of love and desire. If the "we" were merely a derivative experience, the experience of community might enable Sartre to move from the antagonistic view of love as a concrete relation with others to a more communal, nonantagonistic view of love, perhaps a view similar to the one suggested by Goetz in *The Devil and the Good Lord*: "to love anyone is to hate the same enemy."[9]

The "we" is not just a derivative experience, however. It is, in addition, an experience Sartre describes as "of the psychological order and not ontological," as a "pure psychological, subjective event in a single consciousness."[10] Inasmuch as the "we" is merely a derivative *and* subjective relation, it could never offer sufficient resolution of or an alternative to a primitive, ontological antagonism between individuals, such as that found in the circle of concrete relations with others. A derivative, subjective "we" can offer only temporary respite, a brief distraction, from what Iris Murdoch has called the "battle between two hypnotists in a closed room."[11]

If this were a complete and exhaustive analysis of the "we," the conclusion that Sartre has subjectivized such human relationships would seem inescapable. There would be little place for work and communal activity that does any more than leave the human situation as alienated, as objectified and dehumanized as it was found. Reform, rebellion, and revolution would indeed be Quixotic enterprises. Merleau-Ponty would be right, that "for Sartre, the social remains the relationship of 'two individual consciousnesses' which look at each other."[12]

To advance this discussion of the "we," the *Critique of Dialectical Reason* must put forth a different strategy. In *Being and Nothingness* the "we" has so little to offer because it is psychological, not ontological; it is a "purely subjective impression which engages only me."[13] It is fleeting, transitory; it lacks objectivity. It is a freedom without facticity, a purely subjective, fleeting feeling. If the "we" is to be placed on a different footing (indeed, if it is to be placed on a footing at all) in the *Critique*, work must be emphasized and the accomplishment of the "we" recognized. Whereas in *Being and Nothingness* Sartre says "there is no symmetry between the making proof of the Us-object and the experience of the We-subject," the *Critique* would have to discover at least a partial symmetry.[14]

In *Being and Nothingness,* Sartre provides a suggestion of the direction this could take. Here, he recognizes those individuals made into an us-object as
reacting in shame to the third party's look, a look that
reveals their object-side to them. Individuals made
into an us-object become aware of their object-sides in
much the same way a solitary individual becomes
aware of his or her object-side: in each case the look of
another reveals the object-side, and the experience of
the object-side is identified by Sartre in both cases as
"shame." In both cases, shame—an "authentic attitude" toward the other—reveals a dimension of true
existence. Shame, however, is not the only authentic
attitude Sartre recognizes. The other is arrogance: the
affirmation of my freedom confronting the Other-as-
object."[15] If something resembling arrogance could be
found on the side of the we-subject, then at least a partial symmetry would have been discovered between
the experience of the we-subject and the individual's
experience of her or his own freedom. Hence, the we-
subject could not so easily be dismissed as merely the
psychological experience of a single "out of reach and
radically separated" subjectivity.[16]

That is precisely what the *Critique* does. In it, Sartre
develops the notion of "facticity" in some new directions. One of these developments is an emphasis on
social dimensions embedded in an individual's facticity. While the emphasis on these dimensions is new
in the *Critique,* their recognition is not. Sartre's early
discussions of the homosexual and the Jew already involve such recognition. Moreover, in an insert for *The
Age of Reason* and *The Reprieve,* Sartre writes: "The
individual, without ceasing to be a monad, becomes
aware that he is playing a more than individual game.
He is still a window on the world, but he discovers
unexpectedly that his life is taking on a general mean-

ing and coming apart at the seams. It's a monad which has sprung a leak, and which will always keep on leaking even though it will not sink."[17]

In the *Critique*, the social dimensions of facticity are developed along the lines of class differences and conflict. For example, Sartre describes himself watching two laborers at work on either side of a wall. Though not perceived by either laborer, Sartre experiences their work as constituting him as "definite ignorance, as inadequacy." As he says, "I *sense* myself as an intellectual through the limits which they prescribe to my perception," noting that labor is not just a relation between human beings and the material world but "as much a relation between men."[18] As a "relation between men" and as revealing one's facticity or object-side, labor parallels "the look" of *Being and Nothingness*.

What is revealed by labor is one's class-being. Sartre's treatment in the *Critique* of this aspect of facticity differs markedly from that of *Being and Nothingness*. Sartre himself stresses this difference. In his existential writings he denies the a priori existence of essences. By behaving in certain ways, one makes oneself a coward or a thief. Membership in a class, however, is not like being a thief or a coward; it more closely resembles having a withered arm, another of Sartre's early illustrations of facticity. True, one makes oneself a bourgeois as one makes oneself have a withered arm—by interpreting, taking attitudes toward, and living these factors. As Sartre says, though, "in order to make oneself bourgeois, one must be bourgeois."[19] One who is out of work is free; but, as Sartre cautions elsewhere, this does not mean that "he can do whatever he wants and change himself into a rich and tranquil bourgeois on the spot. *He is free because he can always choose to accept his lot with resignation or*

to *rebel against it.*"[20] This is also true of having a withered arm, even of being a waiter, as Sartre earlier recognized. The difference between being a bourgeois or a
waiter and having a withered arm is that the "passive
syntheses of materiality" that exist at the origin of
class membership "are simply the *crystallised practice*
of previous generations: individuals find an existence
already sketched out for them at birth; they 'have their
position in life and their personal development assigned to them by their class.'"[21]

In *The Chips Are Down*, an early play, Sartre recognizes the limiting features of class. As Eve Charlier and
Pierre Dumaine meet among the dead, Pierre mur-
mers, "If I had only met you before." Eve asks what he
would have done; Pierre starts to answer, but "the
words die on his lips." They watch an elegant, pretty
young woman with a poodle on a leash step out of a
chauffeured limousine. She passes a young workman
carrying an iron pipe on his shoulder. As they pass
without even looking at each other, Pierre recognizes
the class differences that separate and make them invisible to each other. To Eve he observes, "She is your
kind, only not as good as you. And he is my kind . . .
not as good as me, either."[22]

Membership in a class assigns one a position and delineates one's possibilities. In this respect it is unlike a
physical attribute such as a withered arm, which may
or may not be a disability, depending on what one tries
to do and what attitudes one takes toward it. Sartre
would no doubt recognize that human *praxis*[23]—pro-
ductive activity—may and often does attach a similar
destiny to aspects of facticity, such as withered arms
and sexual characteristics. In fact, early in his career
Sartre detailed the way in which anti-Semitic *praxis*
has created such a destiny for the Jew.[24] Similarly, in
Cahiers, he depicts a "society of oppression" as one in

which "the concrete ensemble of possibilities [which] determines the field of my freedom . . . is blocked by prohibitions." If one were a solitary freedom, one could simply make possibilities appear. Because, however, a human being is not a solitary freedom, others may determine one's freedom "negatively by possibilities that sketch a concrete geography of freedom and which at the same time are not one's possibilities."[25]

In becoming aware of this inertia created by human *praxis*, human beings are revealed to themselves as related. *Class-being* "defines itself for everyone as an inert (untranscendable) relation with his class comrades on the basis of certain structures. Destiny, general (and even particular) Interest, Exigency, Class Structures, Values as common limits, all necessarily direct our attention not only to a type of individual being . . . but also, through it, to *a type of collective being* as the basis of all individual reality."[26] This class-being, this inertia created by human *praxis*, is therefore the practico-inert limit to their relation and constitutes its objective being. This practico-inert aspect of class-being enables us to understand how, as Sartre recognizes in *Being and Nothingness*, members of an oppressed class can experience themselves in shame as an "us." Moreover, it is "at the heart" of this passivity and inertia characterizing a class that the members of a class can unite and actually negate its passivity.

The notion of facticity is affected the most, however, by the emphasis on scarcity in the *Critique*. To consider the other in the context of scarcity materializes the threat thereof. What was a threat to the way one sees oneself now becomes a threat to one's very existence. In the milieu of scarcity, an individual discovers, *"There is not enough for everybody."* This means "the *mere existence* of everyone is defined by scarcity as the

138

constant danger of non-existence *both for another and for everyone*. Better still: this constant danger of the annihilation of myself and of everyone is not something I see only in *Others*. *I am myself* that danger in so far as I am Other, and designated by the material reality of the environment as potentially surplus *with Others*."[27]

The threat of scarcity emphasizes the embodiment of freedom just as class-being emphasizes the social embeddedness of freedom. Both emphases found in the *Critique* are missing from *Being and Nothingness*. In the *Critique*, Sartre rejects the Stoics' claim that human beings are free in all situations; he says, "I mean the exact opposite: all men are slaves insofar as their life unfolds in the practico-inert field and insofar as this field is always conditioned by scarcity." This means that there is "real subservience to 'natural' forces, to 'mechanical' forces, and to 'anti-social' apparatuses [such that] . . . everyone struggles against an order which really and materially crushes his body and which he sustains and strengthens by his individual struggle against it."[28] Thus, in the *Critique*, a genuine threat to one's existence replaces the merely objectifying look of *Being and Nothingness*. Some have taken this as a rejection of Sartre's existential account of freedom.[29] Those who make such claims, however, tend to ignore what Sartre says about facticity in that existential account. Those who struggle manifest their freedom, as Sartre recognized in his early essay "Materialism and Revolution," even though oppression—and the scarcity recognized in the *Critique*— may leave them "no choice other than resignation or revolution."[30]

Nor is there evidence that Sartre ever associated freedom with a disembodied, unencumbered, totally unrestricted freedom to do anything and everything, pure freedom of the will (explicitly rejected by Sartre in "Materialism and Revolution") or solitary freedom (explicitly rejected in *Cahiers*, another early work). The freedom Sartre long recognized is a freedom that is embodied, frequently oppressed, and which, as a result, may face bleak alternatives. He consistently rejected the self-deception involved in the refusal to see freedom in situations of oppression. As Sartre wrote in *Cahiers*, this is an "ontological mystification" since "ontologically, I have the choice between resignation which is an installation in me of the freedom of the other and the refusal which is merely symbolic and which makes me measure my impotence." The choice between these alternatives is free albeit bleak: "Freedom is free to choose the sauce with which it will be eaten." Real as opposed to symbolic revolt presupposes conditions appertaining which are beyond an individual's control.[31] That is why, in his Introduction to *Les Temps Modernes*, Sartre proposes that "man as we conceive him" is a "free man who must be *delivered*, by widening his possibilities of choice. In certain situations, there is only room for one alternative, one term of which is death. It must be so that man can choose life, in any circumstances."[32]

Even Sartre's characterization of existentialism as an "ideology" should not be read as rejection of his earlier view of freedom. Rather, existentialism is characterized as a "parasitical system living on the margin of Knowledge"—it gets its "nourishment from the living thought of the great dead." Among the "great dead" whose ideas sustain existentialism is, first and foremost, Karl Marx. And it is ultimately some form of Marxism into which existentialism today "seeks to be integrated."[33] This, then, is a use of *ideology* that differs considerably from the one Marxists are familiar with, since, as McBride observes, Sartre clearly is affirming that existentialism is "at least a large fragment of important and otherwise neglected truth."[34] To characterize existentialism as an ideology is anything but an unqualified rejection of existentialism and certainly cannot be read as a rejection of Sartre's earlier view of freedom.

According to the *Critique*, a person exists with others in collectives. Sartre's analyses of various collectives are interesting and illuminating: individuals queuing up at a bus stop, people listening to a radio broadcast, participants in a free-market economy. Like class-being, collectivities impose imperatives on us that relate us to others, but we exist in these relations serially, that is, as each separate from and other than the others. As an "atomised crowd," everybody is designated, and at the same time nobody is. The broadcaster's voice, for example, addresses everyone and no one. There are other listeners, but we are all isolated from each other. An individual's reaction of impotence to a radio broadcast does not result simply from the fact that he or she cannot silence the voice but also because he or she cannot convince "*one by one*, the listeners all of whom it [the voice] exhorts in the common isolation which it creates for all of them as their inert bond."[35] This seriality suggests a type of alienation that is inevitable even in Marxist society.[36] As Sartre says, his impotence "reverts to me and makes *these Others* my destiny."[37]

Earlier in the *Critique*, prior to the discussion of people in collectives, Sartre discusses a clearly inevitable form of alienation arising from the fact that *praxis* as an action on a passive materiality requires "man to objectify himself in a milieu which is not his own and to treat an organic totality [his body] as his objective reality." In acting on the world, one objectifies oneself and must recognize oneself in that objectification; yet, at the same time, one cannot do this. Inasmuch as the result manifests an objectivity, an independence from the agent, and is at least partly shaped by others and by forces over which one has no control, it is both what one did and not what one intended. Sartre indicates that this alienation is traceable to "the very structure of action as the organisation of the unorganised [which] primarily relates the For-itself to its alienated being and Being in itself."[38]

Although action is conscious of itself, actors nevertheless are what they have done (as well as their bodies, their general situations, and the ways in which others see them). They are what they have done, Sartre says; but this aspect of themselves "eludes" them while constituting them as other. This explains why "man *projects himself* in the milieu of the In-Itself-For-Itself," why, that is, being human is the desire to be God. By acting, individuals try to unite themselves with the aspect of themselves that is objectified, with the aspect that seems to be a part of the in-itself. Because such unification is not possible, their alienation from themselves is "fundamental": "Fundamental alienation does not derive, as *Being and Nothingness* might mislead one into supposing, from some prenatal choice: it derives from the univocal relation of interiority which unites man as a practical organism with his environment."[39]

This "fundamental alienation" is an ineradicable aspect of human existence; it may be overcome momentarily but never permanently. An example of momentary overcoming on the social level is what Sartre calls the "group in fusion." Here, there is a spontaneous action of many as one. The oppressed may suddenly rise against their oppressors. They may act and even triumph, but inevitably they fall back into the alterity—the otherness—of the collective. Another example—on the individual rather than the social level—is found in Sartre's novel, *Iron in the Soul*, where Mathieu finds his killing of a Nazi soldier a momentary overcoming of his alienation: "Mathieu looked at the dead soldier and laughed. For years he had tried, in vain, to act. One after the other his intended actions had been stolen from him: he had been no firmer than a pat of butter. But no one had stolen this! He had pressed the trigger, and , for once, something had happened, something definite."[40] He continues to fire from the parapet: "Each one of his shots avenged some ancient scruple. One for Lola whom I dared not rob; one for Marcelle whom I ought not to have left in the lurch; one for Odette whom I didn't want to kiss. This for the books I never dared to write, this for the journeys I never made, this for everybody in general whom I wanted to hate and tried to understand. . . . He fired. He was cleansed. He was all-powerful. He was free."[41]

Fundamental alienation, which can be overcome only momentarily, must be distinguished from both the self-imposed alienation of bad faith and "alienation in the Marxist sense," which "begins with exploitation."[42] It must be distinguished as well from the alienation by abstraction and universality that results from bureaucratic and technological oppression.[43] A person has needs and reduces herself or himself to a "controlled inertia" in order to act on inertia and to satisfy these needs. Individuals want to change the world, to overcome scarcity. Thus they make themselves instruments. They identify with their bodies, alienate themselves from themselves in this fundamental sense.[44] The situation of the oppressed laborer, however, is infected not merely by this fundamental alienation, which pervades all labor and is presupposed by other less fundamental, less benign forms of alienation; the oppressed laborer's situation is, in addition, more extreme. Such laborers work to satisfy their needs; but their labor power has become a commodity; each "turn[s] himself into an inorganic means to an end which has nothing to do with him, rather than an exterior materiality in which he might objectify himself." Workers do not objectify themselves in the machine; rather, "the machine objectifies itself in the worker."[45] Further, their work does not succeed in satisfying their needs, but, on the contrary, exhausts them and ultimately eliminates them by contributing to the development of machines that eventually replace them.[46] For Sartre, this sort of alienation is not benign; neither is it fundamental to human existence.

In recognizing the alienation produced by such work, Sartre, in the *Critique*, seems to continue an opposition to Hegel expressed earlier in *Cahiers*. In the latter, Sartre objects to Hegel's claim that, through the slave's work for the master, the slave becomes conscious of his freedom. For Sartre, the kind of work the slave is forced to do depersonalizes rather than leads to an awareness of freedom. Not only is his work forced, but also the product of his work is doubly stolen from him: "stolen at first because the product is *anonymous* and because it sends back the anonymity to that which produces it (this is totally true only of capitalist oppression); stolen then because its product arises in the field prohibited to the freedom of the worker. . . . [H]e produces a possibility for the others, something impossible for him; he contributes to maintaining the taboos which crisscross the field of his freedom."[47]

Although the slave's work returns to him an image of his activity and thus to that degree may be liberating, it is, according to Sartre, misery, dependence, and hunger that are the "true liberating elements." Fear is not included in this list, since, Sartre argues: "The

144

slave born in the mansion does not fear for his life as Hegel supposes in referring to the prisoner of war."[48] Instead, the fact that the slave has a destiny like that of a thing between the hands of the master, the order of dependence, "replaces this fear by the enduring contradiction between a freedom that is not able to prevent itself from projecting its own future and the perpetual disarming of this freedom by the altering freedom of the Other."[49] It is just such unnecessary alienation that Sartre's Marxism is primarily concerned with eliminating. This alienation is overcome when the workers become aware of the "opaque materiality of impotence and inertia" that is their class-being, then move from passive recognition to action, to *praxis*, to negate this class-being. In other words, in the language of *Being and Nothingness*, they must first become aware of themselves as an us-object and then act as a we-subject. They become a group in fusion as was accomplished, according to Sartre, by the Parisians who moved from suffering in impotence to storming the Bastille.[50] For the moment they become a purely active class, integrating all its members into a single *praxis*, something realized, as Sartre notes, "only in very rare (and revolutionary) moments of working-class history."[51]

It is in his account of the activity of the we-subject— the group in fusion in particular but also the statutory group, the organization, and the institution—that Sartre's view in the *Critique* goes beyond what he says of the we-subject in *Being and Nothingness*. In the first place, the *Critique* emphasizes work. The "we" is not merely subjective; like an individual who acts, it has an object-side. In labor, the individual "is reduced to inorganic materiality in order to act materially on matter and to change his material life." A similar moment of adopted inertia is the necessary condition for common action.[52] This recognition is central to Sartre's unfolding of the constituted dialectic, the dynamics of the group. Since the group, unlike the individual, is not an organism, it must create this inertia if it is to make common action possible. This is the problem that faces the group, and it is resolved as each individual moves from being an "alienating Third" (like the Third described in *Being and Nothingness*, whose look leads to the experience of an "us") to being a "regulating Third," assuming "responsibility for the praxis of the others by designating his own action regulative of the common action, and this prior to any formal organization of the group."[53]

The group, existing somewhere between the seriality of the collective and the unity of the organism, is haunted by an impossible ideal, just as the individual of *Being and Nothingness* is haunted by the in-itself and by the impossible desire to be God. For the group as for the individual, the unity sought cannot be attained. There is an important difference, however: the group is not an individual, and the adopted inertia of the group prevents common praxis from having the same translucidity as individual praxis. My right and my duty, insofar as I am a member of the group, "appear with a dimension of alterity . . . as my free alienation from my freedom."[54] Unlike the alterity that arises, in F.H. Bradley's idealism, between the individual and his or her station and its duties, there is no ultimate unity in which this otherness will be dialectically overcome.[55] This explains the fact that, for the group, the impossible ideal of organic unity changes into the idea of practical organism, "which becomes regulatory by constantly positing itself as capable of being realised the next day."[56] Thus, as Flynn recognizes, collective responsibility becomes an "ideal in the Kantian sense": "As Sartre achieved a practical 'synthesis' of self and other in the group, so it is precisely as a practical ideal that collective responsibility can bridge the gap which he observes between praxis and the purely imaginary."[57]

The most important difference between *Being and Nothingness* and the *Critique* is that, according to the latter, individuals with needs in a context of scarcity need not react merely as individuals in shame or in arrogance as they become aware of themselves as oppressed; they can join together in action. For example, they can storm the Bastille. They may, however, then disperse and once again exist serially. Neither the fact that they have acted nor the objective accomplishment to which they can point is in itself sufficient to hold the group together so that further common action is possible; yet a need for common action often persists. For example, the retreated enemy may return. To keep itself ready for action, the group imposes the oath on itself, and fraternity/terror results. The group differentiates in order to unify: "through a pledge, freedom gives itself a practical certainty for cases in which (because circumstances vary) future behavior is unpredictable."[58] Through this pledge, a bond of fraternity is produced; at the same time, terror comes into being inasmuch as the pledge affirms the right of the group over an individual's praxis.[59]

The unity produced by the pledge is precarious; thus, to expel the freedom that constantly threatens the continued existence of the group, the institution arises. An authority emerges as an "individual reincarnation of the fused group and of Freedom-Terror." Because of their pledged faith, it will appear legitimate to those within the state, but not to those outside.[60]

Sartre notes the "contradictions" in each of these attempts to create the group as a unity, indicating that inevitably there is a lapse back into seriality: "sooner or later they [groups] return to the statute of inertia."[61] There are, he says, limits to the group's praxis:

> born to dissolve series in the living synthesis of a community, it is blocked in its spatio-temporal development by the untranscendable statute of organic individuality and finds its being, outside itself, in the passive determinations of inorganic exteriority which it had wished to repress in itself. It is formed in opposition to alienation, in so far as alienation substitutes the practico-inert field for the free practical field of the individual; but it cannot escape alienation any more than the individual can, and it thereby lapses into serial passivity.[62]

Thus the group comes into being as an attempt to overcome alienation, but it cannot escape alienation; it founders instead on the ineradicable individuality and freedom of its members. Far from being deliberately rejected by the *Critique*, the individual plays a central and vital role in the dialectic developed therein.[63]

The group, then, is neither an individual nor a purely subjective experience; it is an ambiguous sort of existence, an accomplishment to be accomplished. To this extent, it is like cowardice and a withered arm, as Sartre described them in *Being and Nothingness*. Like a withered arm, the practico-inert aspect of the state is (or may be) an element of one's facticity with respect to which—initially, at least—one is passive. Inasmuch as it acts on the world, however, the group is more. The group may come into being as a real, effective response to need in a situation of scarcity, or it may enable us to overthrow oppression and thereby abolish an alienation that can and should be eliminated. Although the group is always subject to destruction, nonetheless it may exist for a time and act. Unlike cynicism, the group is not something that immediately effects its undoing. Though inherently unstable, the group may endure long enough to correct part or perhaps all of the oppressive situation against which it first arose.

Thus what the *Critique* offers is an important distinction between kinds of alienation: fundamental alienation is distinguished explicitly from "Marxist" alienation and implicitly from the self-imposed alienation of bad faith. As Pietro Chiodi has recognized, Sartre thereby avoids the Hegelian optimism of complete overcoming of alienation. Sartre avoids as well, as Chiodi acknowledges but somehow fails sufficiently to credit, a simple Hegelian identification of alienation and objectification.[64] Indeed, Sartre recognizes that "alienation in the Marxist sense begins with exploitation," asking: "[Should we] go back to Hegel who sees alienation as a constant characteristic of all kinds of objectification?" He answers his own question: "Yes and no. We must recognize that the original relation between *praxis* as totalisation and materiality as passivity obliges man to objectify himself in a milieu which is not his own, and to treat an organic totality as his objective reality."[65]

Fundamental alienation may be identified more or less with objectification—in being, in the consequences of one's actions, in and through others in society. By recognizing that this fundamental alienation cannot be suppressed, Sartre denies the possibility of a completely overcoming alienation and separates himself from what Chiodi sees as the "Marxism of today"—"an 'idealistic voluntarism'—a form of terrorism operating from Hegelian premises."[66] The form of Marxism Sartre advocates would accept the antinomy "which constitutes the problem of ethics": "If I take the freedom of the other as my objective goal, I do him violence. But if I take my own freedom as my goal, it involves requiring all the others to be free. In the choice I make of my freedom, the freedom of the others is demanded; but when I move to the level of action, I have to take the other person as a means and not as an end."[67] The kind of alienation Sartre is concerned to eliminate is the alienation resulting from oppression, not from objectification. Early in his career—in *Cahiers*, in fact—Sartre proposed that the root of oppression is desire, not objectification. Desire, an origin of magic, like action at a distance, constitutes itself as a right: "the stronger the desire, the more the object *ought* to fulfill it." Desire rather than objectification leads to oppression, since "in the world of desire the object is considered essential and man inessential."[68]

Because Sartre distinguishes kinds of alienation, he can criticize societies in a number of ways. First, because he denies that fundamental alienation can be overcome, Sartre can criticize societies that fail to acknowledge this fact, just as he criticizes individuals in bad faith for failure to acknowledge their facticity. Although both societies and individuals are haunted by ideals of unifications they cannot attain, a society that operates on this "idealistic voluntarism" is like individuals who refuse their past, their facticity, their being-for-others. Such a society, like Garcin in *No Exit*, in effect, claims that willing makes it so: "A man is what he wills to be."[69]

In addition, by recognizing forms of alienation that are eliminable, Sartre can criticize societies that oppress, just as he criticizes individuals, such as the anti-Semite, who oppress others and deny their freedom. Societies, like individuals, seek a unity that cannot be attained; thus there is a sense in which all societies, like all individuals, are on a par: they all fail. Yet, like individuals, societies can play "loser wins." Societies and individuals can move from impossible ideals posited absolutely and idealistically to the same ideals posited regulatively or playfully.[70] Thus they win by overcoming that alienation which can be overcome. Within themselves and by their actions, they create syntheses, albeit unstable and fleeting, of subjectivity and objectivity. Though not the undifferentiated unities sought, these syntheses, at least for the moment, are temporal, ambiguous intimations of those ultimate but impossible ideals toward which they strive.[71]

Societies, then, can be criticized and may be engaged in something very much like the behavior of individuals in bad faith. To condemn revolution and other attempts to overcome alienation as "Quixotic enterprise[s]" would, for Sartre, itself be a form of bad faith, an attempt to use the inevitability of failure as an excuse, as a justification for any action whatsoever. If all alienation were regarded by Sartre as fundamental, then Meszaros' criticism of other existentialists would also find its mark in Sartre; if all alienation were regarded by Sartre as inevitable, his philosophy would offer a support for the status quo and would render any attempt at a practical transcendence of this alienation a puzzling, Quixotic enterprise. Yet, precisely because not all alienation is fundamental and insurmountable, Sartre can make a judgment—a moral one—condemning societies that oppress and thereby gratuitously alienate classes from one another and individual members of some of those classes from themselves, from the products of their labor, and from each other. He can affirm the class struggle in its effort to loosen the chains with which humans have bound their fellow human beings.[72] As a writer, Sartre may himself try to change this situation by revealing the human race to its members, by provoking the reader's "intention of treating men, in every case, as an absolute end," by directing the reader's attention upon the oppressed of the world, and by showing "that it is quite impossible to treat concrete men as ends in contemporary society."[73]

As Flynn observes, those who find "scandalous" Sartre's overcoming of his dichotomies with only "practical 'syntheses'" are "those whose dialectic is omnivorous; who hope for more than a practical synthesis; who expect to 'subsume' the inert in the spontaneous, immanence in transcendence, the other in the same, and the individual in the social."[74] Such hope and expectation may, in fact, be at the root of the apparent inability, manifest in some otherwise astute critics, to recognize that Sartre proposed such syntheses.

Like the "we" of *Being and Nothingness*, the "we" of the *Critique* does not provide a way of relating to others that will overcome our fundamental alienation from ourselves and from others which we experience through the look, in the successes and failures of our actions, and in the situatedness of our being. Though haunted by unifications we can never attain, we remain divided within ourselves, alienated from being, separated from one another. We cannot escape this fundamental alienation by merging into the unity of a group, since the group itself is problematic: it too is ambiguous; it too seeks a unity it cannot attain.

The experience of the "we" may offer temporary respite from the circle of relations in bad faith as they are described in *Being and Nothingness*. The "we" of the *Critique*, however, offers more; it gives us a way to overcome a particular scarcity or a nonfundamental, eliminable alienation imposed by some people on others. The *Critique* thereby uses a "we" which, as Sartre observes in *Cahiers*, "becomes real at the anthropological level of the common work." This, Sartre says, is a concrete "we" the object returns to me and ". . . where my *I* establishes itself and loses itself. I return at the same time to my justification and my inexistence as a singular person. Thus, that which is impossible at the level of the For-itself and of the Project (the ontological organization of a We) becomes real at the anthropological level of common work."[75]

In societies, people can engage authentically. In their practical willing of their own freedom and that of others, they , like Genet, may free themselves from ghosts that have haunted them. They may even free themselves from chains, from arbitrary, dehumanizing limitations. If, as Sartre says, Genet becomes a man, perhaps we could say that some societies become humanized.[76]

7

Sequestration and Love

... when I met Simone de Beauvoir,
I felt I had found the best
relationship that I could ever have
with anyone. The most complete
relationship. I'm not talking about
sex or about intimacy, but rather
about conversations on the vital
decisions in our life. Indeed, a
relationship of such completeness
made for a profound equality
between us.
　　　—Sartre, *Playboy*, December 1977

In *Being and Nothingness*, Sartre affirms that all actions are equivalent "Thus it amounts to the same thing whether one gets drunk alone or is a leader of nations."[1] This remark has been erroneously interpreted by many of his critics and even by some of his admirers to mean that Sartre's notion of authenticity is totally individualistic and compatible with any and all behavior toward others. This misinterpretation is reinforced by many of Sartre's own analyses—for example, his circle of concrete relations with others and his many plays, novels, and short stories, the central characters of which are loners, individuals cut off from others, usually by their own doing.

Self-sequestration and its narcissistic individualism may well have been one of Sartre's greatest personal temptations. In *The Words* he affirms that his "natural place" is a "sixth floor in Paris with a view overlooking the roofs," with "the Universe" rising "in tiers" at his feet, all things "humbly beg[ging] for a name," begging to be created and taken. Also in *The Words*, Sartre notes his negative reaction to a heroism that had been put "within the reach of everyone." What he preferred, Sartre admits, was not "community victories" but the "solitude and gratuitousness" of prewar heroism.[2] While Sartre admits that he was Roquentin, gaily demonstrating in *Nausea* that "man is impossible,"[3] he is also the writer who praises Goetz's involvement in good and evil: "[Goetz] discovers the way of human truth. . . . In this way [Goetz] discovers his moral law: separation is real and absolute unity is necessary. Here again we meet the express fact that the individual is the goal of the collectivity and at the same time the collectivity is the goal of the individual."[4] Sartre may have been Roquentin, but it seems just as true, as de Beauvoir wrote, that Goetz is the individual Sartre would have liked to be.[5]

Contrary to the way Sartre saw himself, Goetz is far closer to the man Sartre actually was. Sartre argued for and lived the role of the committed writer. In *What Is Literature?* he says: "To reveal is to change" and "the writer has chosen to reveal the world and particularly to reveal man to other men so that the latter may assume full responsibility before the object which has thus been laid bare."[6] Although Sartre, like Roquentin, for some time may have taken his role as a writer as a way to justify himself, to become essential, he finally lost such illusions yet continued to write even while recognizing that culture "doesn't save anything or anyone, it doesn't justify. But it is a product of man: he projects himself into it, he recognizes himself in it; that critical mirror alone offers him his image."[7] Sartre wrote about man and human freedom. He sought to reveal and to change. Certainly he was a committed writer.

In his writings Sartre depicts numerous types and instances of bad faith, some primarily solitary, some involving others. He argues that we should will and actively support the freedom of all human beings. He maintains that without objective changes in society it is impossible to treat others as ends. Positive models for respecting, loving relationships are rare, as the foregoing would lead one to suspect, though not as rare as critics would have us believe. In particular, two individuals stand out: Hoederer and Genet. They, however, can best be understood by contrast with those who sequester themselves and reject relationships of love and respect with their fellows.

Sequestration takes many different forms in Sartre's writings. Some are sequestered voluntarily. For example, in *The Condemned of Altona*, Franz sequesters himself in the family mansion, in particular walling out his father and post-war Germany (which Franz desperately wants to believe is writhing in agony under the heavy, relentless foot of occupation forces). In "The Room," Eve tries, albeit unsuccessfully, to shut herself off from the uncomprehending world of normal people and to enter into the insane world of her husband, Pierre. Unable to believe in Pierre's hallucinations or even to stifle a suspicion that his tortures are self-inflicted and freely assented to, Eve accepts the truth of Pierre's recognition that "There is a wall between you and me." She realizes that she belongs nowhere.[8] Even the members of the ménage à trois in *No Exit* sequester themselves inasmuch as no one leaves when the door is opened.

Others are sequestered against their wills. The captives in "The Wall" have been jailed for alleged revolutionary activity. Similarly, Genet, while in prison, is at least physically sequestered.

Some are sequestered by themselves; others are sequestered together. Although we should expect to find rejection of others in any who voluntarily sequester themselves from all others, it is more difficult to anticipate the attitudes of those who sequester themselves with others. Among Sartre's characters who sequester themselves with others, it is clear that most of them are rejecting their own freedom and that of others. For example, Garcin and Estelle, in *No Exit*, deny their own freedom and responsibility, and in the process each is profoundly threatened by the look and freedom of others. In *The Condemned of Altona*, Franz admits one other person into his retreat: his sister, Leni. Leni, who loves and willingly involves herself in an incestuous relationship with her brother, enters his seclusion at some cost. She must deny to Franz much that she knows to be true, and she must profess what she knows to be false. When Leni tries to protect Franz from an intrusion she knows will destroy their relationship, that will likely destroy him too, he responds: "You bore me."[9] Franz, busy making tapes he hopes will justify him, his comrades, and his age before the tribunal of the future, is too uncomfortable with his own freedom to take seriously another's freedom. Thus the only person to whom he can relate is a sister, someone more like a part of himself, one who is not wholly another.[10]

In *Dirty Hands*, Hugo tries through revolutionary activity to escape from himself. His activity is wholly negative, however; it is always in opposition to something. Thus he never feels a part of situations when he is with others. Hugo is not one of the dispossessed; he is not acting on behalf of their freedom. On the contrary, he is merely trying to negate his past as he acts on behalf of an abstract freedom that actually is no one's. He seems at ease only when he is alone or with his wife Jessica in their room with his middle-class memories (snapshots of himself in a velvet jacket, of himself with a sailor collar and a beret) and with the symbol of his role in the revolution: his gun. Even Hugo and Jessica seem little more than reflections of each other. Neither, for example, can say to the other with any conviction, "I love you." When Hoederer asks Jessica if she and Hugo love each other, she responds, "Not even. We're too much alike." Neither Hugo nor Jessica can do more than play at being serious, at believing each other.[11]

Similarly, numerous characters sequestered by others are unwilling to recognize and accept their own freedom and that of others. For example, Pablo Ibbieta ("The Wall"), though possessing a remarkable degree of lucidity, appears to be in bad faith. He has been active in the resistance in Spain against Franco. Under the watchful eye of his captors, he more or less limits his action to what is under his control: to be awake and alert as he is taken before the firing squad the next morning. Yet, just before his captors come for him at dawn, the rejection of his freedom and responsibility is manifest. Under sentence of death all night, Pablo lost the illusion of immortality. Along with that illusion vanished all the significance he once attached to his revolutionary activity as well as his concern for and commitment to his girlfriend. Still, he continues to look for significance, for friendship, love, and commitment to a cause, as though these have objective reality. Thus Pablo discovers that it makes no difference whether he or Gris or somebody else is shot, that "no life has value," that "nothing [is] important."[12] Although Pablo has lost his illusion that values are objective, nonetheless he is not ready to assume his responsibility for their existence.

Involuntary sequestration and torture have a similar effect on Lucie's love for Jean in *Men Without Shad-*

ows. Jean and Lucie are imprisoned with several of their comrades. Jean, the leader of the insurrectionary group, was captured separately, and his captors do not suspect he has any connection with the others; in fact, the others are being tortured for information concerning Jean. A triangle of sorts develops as Henri, one of the comrades, confesses his love for Lucie, "because it doesn't matter any more." Lucie allows Henri to kill her young brother François who, they fear, under torture will reveal Jean's identity. Their shame and suffering bring Lucie and Henri together and separate them from Jean. When Jean reminds Lucie that their love was their whole life, she responds: "Our life, yes. Our future. I lived in an eternal expectation. I loved you in expectation. I was waiting for the end of the war. Waiting for the day when we could be married in the eyes of the world. Each night I waited for you. Now I have no future. I expect nothing but my death, and I shall die alone. . . . Leave me alone. We have nothing to say to each other. I am not in pain and I have no need for consolation." Like Pablo, Lucie has lived in an illusion of immortality. When that is destroyed, all she has left is her pride: "All that I want is for them to come for me again, and to beat me, so that I can keep silent again, and fool them and frighten them."[13]

While these examples reinforce the view that Sartre's position allows only a "perpetual hopeless struggle of each against the other," other examples indicate more positive possibilities for human relationships.[14] The following seem especially significant: the relationships of Genet and his readers, of Eve and Pierre *(The Chips Are Down)*, of Hoederer and Hugo *(Dirty Hands)*, of Hilda and Goetz *(The Devil and the Good Lord)*, and of Anna and Kean *(Kean)*.

Admittedly Genet's stance vis-à-vis his readers does not qualify as a personal relationship with them. I mention it again to call attention to features that seem necessary to respecting, loving relationships. Though incarcerated, Genet writes for those from whom he is physically sequestered. Examined from the perspective of *What Is Literature?* Genet appears the writer par excellence. He writes to reveal man and to change his readers—and he succeeds. He accepts his own freedom and addresses himself to the freedom of others. He addresses them as free in order to free them and himself. In the process, all, including Genet, are transformed.

In a sense, Eve Charlier and Pierre Dumaine are sequestered initially in *The Chips Are Down.* In their netherworld of the dead, they at least are separated from the living, from the others they love. They are given the opportunity to return to life, to try to love each other "with perfect coincidence and with all their . . . might."[15] They do love each other, but when they rejoin the living they are torn by other loves and loyalties. Pierre tries to save his comrades from staging an insurrection that will be only a trap for them. Eve is concerned about her sister, Lucette, whom André, Eve's husband, is trying to win over so that, after Eve's death, he can marry Lucette for her dowry, just as he earlier married Eve for hers.

Unable to love each other with perfect confidence and not even the slightest of misgivings, Eve and Pierre return to the dead. There they meet two young people who, like Eve and Pierre earlier, have discovered they were made for each other and who seek the opportunity to live their lives over. Eagerly they ask Pierre and Eve if they really can try to live their lives over. Pierre and Eve respond with odd looks and gentle smiles. "Try," Pierre advises. "Try it anyway," murmurs Eve.[16]

Although Sartre admits that he was having fun here with a nonexistential determinism (in which the chips are down and lovers are meant for one another), the play itself does suggest a couple of points with respect to love.[17] First, a love of perfect coincidence, of perfect confidence and no misgivings, is presented as an impossibility, given the ambiguous creatures human beings are. This recognition should surprise neither Sartre's critics nor his admirers; what may surprise both critics and admirers is the affirmation of the attempt to love with perfect coincidence, an affirmation that emerges in Eve's and Pierre's replies to the young aspiring lovers. There is a wistfulness in their responses, but there is more: a recognition in their urging of the importance of the attempt even though it cannot succeed.

Hoederer's relationship with Hugo is quite revealing, too. At his own peril, Hoederer recognizes Hugo's difficulty in growing out of his middle-class childhood and becoming a revolutionary. Hoederer respects Hugo's freedom and risks his own life in order to help Hugo grow up. Realizing that Hugo has been sent as an assassin, Hoederer nevertheless gives Hugo numerous opportunities to complete his mission. Hoederer trusts Hugo even though it may (and eventually does) mean Hoederer's own death. It is only when Hugo finds Jessica and Hoederer embracing that Hugo shoots Hoederer. Even then, Hoederer tries to protect Hugo by telling the guards that he had been sleeping with Hugo's wife.

In the plays *The Devil and the Good Lord* and *Kean*, Sartre develops two other characters who, like Hoederer, love without being loved in turn and who also love clear-sightedly, nonpossessively, and without bad faith. In *The Devil and the Good Lord*, Hilda is loved by the peasants because, as she says, she "needs" them. Goetz resolves to rescue the peasants' love for himself by having Hilda love him. Goetz achieves their love and improves their lot but in the process corrupts Hilda, who recognizes that she has "less love for [the peasants] since they have less suffering." Recognizing Goetz's misery, Hilda stays with him, later confessing to Heinrich that she loves Goetz while acknowledging only that Goetz "has loved me as much as he has loved himself."[18]

Against Goetz's fear of "coupling in public" ("under the eyes of God"), Hilda responds that love is a "deep night" that hides lovers from God's regard: "when people love each other, they become invisible to God." In response to Goetz's horror of sexual love ("how can I desire to hold in my arms this bag of excrement?"), she assures him, "[if] you die, I will lie down beside you and stay there to the very end, without eating or drinking; you will rot away in my embrace, and I will love your carrion flesh; for *you do not love at all, if you do not love everything.*"[19]

Finally, Hilda loves without idealizing. She recognizes that Goetz "will never be like other men. Neither better nor worse: different."[20]

McMahon proposes that Anna in *Kean* is a "new kind of character in Sartre's work." From the previous analyses of Hoederer and Hilda, it is clear that the kind of character Anna represents is not especially new in Sartre's work; but McMahon is correct in recognizing her importance in Sartre's theory of love.[21]

Anna has fallen in love with the actor Kean, whom she observed through many performances. When Kean, assuming he has impressed her with his performances, seeks to shock and disillusion her by informing her that he was "drunk as an Irish lord," she indicates that she was quite aware of that fact, and acknowledges his various errors: calling other actors by the wrong name, inserting moving soliloquies from other plays. Mystified that she knew he was drunk, yet "applauded all the same," Kean is told that she applauded to encourage him and because she knew he must be unhappy.[22]

Anna sees Kean clearly, responding to what she perceives as his need somewhat as Hilda does to the suffering of the peasants and later to Goetz's misery: "So I made enquiries, and I found you were a drunkard, a libertine, crippled with debts, melancholy and mad by turns, and I said to myself: 'That man needs a wife.'" When she recognizes that Solomon, Kean's prompter, also loves Kean, she resolves that "nothing will be changed" and that Solomon should live with her and Kean after they are married. Like Hilda, Anna seems unafraid of the eyes of the other. Finally, as she prepares to leave for America, she seems to accept with good grace the conclusion that Kean does not love her. Although she lies, as she says, to "make" Kean marry her, she nonetheless seems to be as clear-sightedly aware of Kean's freedom as she is of his character.[23]

Although these examples do not develop all the diverse possibilities of human relationships, they do indicate a broader spectrum of such relationships than scholars usually have found in Sartre's work. In particular, these examples indicate several distinctly different views of love. There is the view of love with which readers of *Being and Nothingness* are familiar. At this level, as Sartre says in *Cahiers*, "[sadism] and masochism are the revelation of the Other." He adds, however, that this sadism and masochism "have meaning . . . only before the conversion."[24] In this type of relationship the lovers are in bad faith and seek to make use of each other in trying to hide their freedom and responsibility from themselves. The lovers seek solitude, Sartre says, because the look of a third party effectively destroys the game they play with each other. Such love requires sequestration.

Second is the love that exists between or among

those who are, as it were, comrades-in-arms. This is the sort of love that is produced by terror, according to the *Critique* ("a practical bond of *love* between the lynchers [or traitors]"), and which Goetz has in mind when he affirms, "To love anyone is to hate the same enemy."[25] It is in terms of this kind of love that Henri and Lucie *(Men Without Shadows)* are drawn closer through their tortured shame and suffering even as they are separated from Jean. Similarly, when Mathieu, in *The Age of Reason*, imitates Ivich's gesture and stabs his own hand, their common defiance of others' opinions momentarily brings them to a sense of intimacy they have not previously experienced and which they do not experience again.[26]

Apparently, Sartre sees opposition as central to love, since, in discussing *The Devil and the Good Lord*, he says, "Broadly speaking this is what I mean. First, every love is in opposition to God. As soon as two people love each other, they love each other in opposition to God. Every love is in opposition to the absolute because it is itself absolute. . . . If God exists, man does not exist; and if man exists, God does not exist."[27] Although love always may be in opposition to God, it is clear from Sartre's examples that it need not be always in opposition to anything else. Pierre and Eve *(The Chips Are Down)* love each other, but they neither have nor hate the same enemy. Similarly, Hoederer's love for Hugo seems not to be connected to hatred of enemies; in fact, even though both are communists and are active in the party, it is not all clear that they hate the same enemy.

What can be seen in the love of Pierre and Eve is recognition of a third kind of love, of human relationships that strive in a positive, authentic way for perfect coincidence, perfect confidence. Such coincidence with another, like that of an individual with herself or himself, cannot be achieved. Ambiguity and a tension of opposites are ineradicably part of the human condition; yet the effort to harmonize and unify the inharmonious and disparate may well be vital to human striving, especially, as we have seen, to authentic striving.

Finally, Hoederer's love for Hugo involves a genuine effort to treat Hugo as an end. At each point his efforts backfire, and Hugo feels insulted—humiliated, made fun of—rather than loved and respected. When Hoederer intervenes and tries to resolve the antagonism between Hugo and Hoederer's bodyguards, Hugo is outraged to find himself defended by Hoederer. Similarly, Hoederer's trust of Hugo, even to the point of giving Hugo the opportunity to fulfill his assignment by assassinating Hoederer, evokes from Hugo the response, "I hate you."[28]

In Hoederer's love for Hugo, Hilda's for Goetz, and Anna's for Kean and in the unsuccessful love of Eve and Pierre, Sartre exemplifies what he recognizes in *What Is Literature?*: "it is quite impossible to treat concrete men as ends in contemporary society." As in the cases of Hoederer and Hugo and of Eve and Pierre, the injustices of the age—class divisions, racism, and so forth—inevitably, Sartre argues, intervene and vitiate "at the roots" the good one strives to accomplish.[29] Similarly, Goetz remains the unlovable bastard, unable to accept himself, desiring only "to be a man among men."[30] He moves only from feeling more alone, the more he is loved, to acknowledging Hilda's love by incorporating her into himself and admitting her to his loneliness: "You are myself. We shall be alone together."[31]

Kean may appear more optimistic, inasmuch as it ends with Kean linking arms with Anna and Solomon and saying, "My true, my only friends."[32] It is difficult, however, not to imagine the future Kean as he tries to make a living in America, whether by acting or not, once again wondering if his action was truly an action or merely a gesture and once again struggling with his existence as a bastard in the eyes of others.[33]

Although it may be impossible today to treat men as ends, nonetheless, according to Sartre in *What Is Literature?*, the writer strives, as does Hoederer, to hold in tension the affirmations of revolution and the kingdom of ends. In the loves exemplified by Hoederer, Hilda, Anna, Pierre, and Eve, ambiguity prevails; failure is inevitable. Nevertheless, they reach beyond such failure.

What is thereby indicated about the possibilities of love is, given Sartre's view of man, freedom, and authenticity, to be expected. There is a kind of love that recognizes and affirms the freedom of both the lover and the beloved. Whatever the features of the human condition or of the social structures created by human activity which render problematic or impossible the expression or realization of such love, the authentic individual must affirm and actively support the freedom of others. Such love goes beyond the sadomasochistic dialectic of enslaving freedoms to a "deeper recognition and reciprocal comprehension of freedoms," a dimension, which Sartre notes in *Cahiers*, is lacking in *Being and Nothingness*. This sort of love "requires the *tension*: to maintain the two faces of the ambiguity, to retain them in the unity of the same project." It is a "completely different thing than the desire to appropriate."[34] Like other authentic activity, authentic relationships with others must maintain a tension between what is sought and what is achieved, between coincidence and inevitable alienation and separateness, between treating the other as an end and treating her or him as a means. Like the writer, though, an authentic individual can approach the other with a confidence concerning human freedom.

Such love may involve all the joy and some of the sorrow depicted in the account of love in *Being and Nothingness*. There, Sartre notes the "basis for the joy of love when there is joy: we feel our existence is justified."[35] This joy bears a strong resemblance to the aesthetic joy Sartre describes in *What Is Literature?*: "identical, at first, with the recognition of a transcendent and absolute end which, for a moment, suspends the utilitarian round of ends-means and means-ends."[36] Aesthetic joy involves recognition on the part of the reader of his or her freedom, and "a consciousness of being essential in relation to an object perceived as essential." Sartre calls this aspect of aesthetic consciousness the "feeling of security," noting that it "stamps the strongest aesthetic emotions with a sovereign calm," and affirms that "it has its origin in the authentication of a strict harmony between subjectivity and objectivity."[37]

Although Sartre loses the illusion that identified him with Roquentin—that, through writing, he could justify his life and become essential—nevertheless he continued to write and, I presume, to experience aesthetic joy. Surely one can say the same thing about love. The authentic individual has lost any illusions of being justified and made essential by another. This individual recognizes his or her own freedom and thereby, if Sartre's analysis in *What Is Literature?* is right, already experiences a kind of joy. Like the writer, the authentic lover can approach the other with confidence in freedom and with a trust and generosity.[38] Aesthetic joy and the joy of love may be momentary; nonetheless, they are intimations of the harmony sought. As momentary, they may bring sorrow and negate the aspirations of those who seek therein to be justified and essential and to escape their freedom and responsibility. For the authentic, however, such intimations may be taken in stride as temporal, albeit fleeting and ambiguous, embodiments of the ultimate but impossible goals toward which they strive. Once again, although what is sought does not change when one becomes authentic, the way it is sought does.

Like Hoederer, those who love are left with "dirty hands" in the sense that they must face the paradox: the only way to treat another as an end is to treat her or him as a means; the only way to respect freedom is to violate it. This paradox is one Sartre makes clear in *Being and Nothingness*, where, in discussing the attempt to act on the precepts of Kantian morality, he notes that respecting the freedom of another may require that one "force" that person to be free. To treat the other with charity or tolerance is to cause her or him "to be thrown forcefully into a tolerant world" and to remove those courageous possibilities of resistance and that would have resulted from a world of intolerance.[39]

This love is not part of a morality that fuses individuals into a single consciousness. In *Cahiers*, Sartre warns against just such a fusion, as well as against a kingdom of ends that recognizes each consciousness only in its Kantian universality. Instead, the morality he approves would take each individual in its "concrete singularity."[40]

At the same time, what Sartre says in *Cahiers* of the parent-child relationship is instructive. This relationship itself is a "situation of violence" inasmuch as even a liberating parent must explain his or her decisions and prohibitions and inasmuch as such attempts to reason with a child are always situations of violence: "one cannot say all the truth to children or . . . one is able to tell them, but they do not comprehend."

The situation becomes one of violence, since "the reason is not *all* the reason." Therefore, in this as in all hierarchies, there is failure. Yet additional violence to the child can be avoided by recognizing that "in each case, the situation of the child is the means for its concrete and real emancipation; it is necessary to see the future from the viewpoint of the present, to understand that it is *the future of this present*; to give an absolute value to each present with the future that it prefigures."[41]

Even when violence is unavoidable or necessary for attaining the end, if the goal is concrete and finite, it ought to exclude violence. Such unavoidable or necessary violence will appear "unjustifiable and *limited*[,] . . . the failure at the heart of the result." The finite end must be present in the means, and the means, without ceasing to be means, will be "at the same time the goal if it participates in the goal (if the ultimate emancipation of man is at the same time the emancipation of each minute. But because it is necessary that the ultimate emancipation be regulative and that in each case the goal be a finite emancipation on a determined point)."[42]

Finally, something must be said about transparency. Just as transparency is important in authenticity vis-à-vis oneself, so, for Sartre, it is vital in friendship, love, and other social relationships. Sartre's affirmation of the significance of transparency to one another to some extent offsets his rejection, in *Being and Nothingness*, of the possibility of treating another as an unconditioned end. This, he says, is impossible, since to treat the other as a goal is to objectify the other's freedom, making it a "transcendence-transcended."[43] This sort of thinking treats subject and object, means and end, as mutually exclusive alternatives, and ultimately it is rejected by Sartre as inappropriate for human beings who are and must be thought of as subjects that are objects, and vice versa, ends that are means, and vice versa.

At any rate, Sartre refers to the "transparency" of his friendship with Merleau-Ponty, a transparency clouded by "small jolts of anger" until they became strangers.[44] They left with nothing "in common but their quarrel." What they lacked, Sartre says, was the "undertaking." Their past activity alone remained but "took its revenge by making us pensioners of friendship."[45]

There is a strong suggestion here that a present activity—a common enemy, as Goetz would say, to rise up against and fight—could have reunited the former friends and once more made them transparent to one another. In an interview late in his life, Sartre denies that today we realize this degree of visibility. The antagonisms among people, which ultimately are traceable to material scarcity, result in a "depth of darkness" in the individual, "things which refuse to be said . . . which resist being said to another."[46] Nevertheless, Sartre goes on to affirm, transparency is necessary "before true social harmony can be established": "A man's existence must be entirely visible to his neighbor, whose own existence must be entirely visible in turn."[47] This perceived importance of visibility to each other gives a perspective from which to interpret the emphasis Sartre has given to methods of disclosing the other: existential psychoanalysis in *Being and Nothingness,* the "existentialist approach" in *Search for a Method,* and the continued effort to understand Flaubert in these works and in the special study, *The Idiot of the Family.*

Whereas emphasis on the importance of transparency to oneself and to others illuminates some of his own work, it remains one of the more problematic aspects of Sartre's ethics. This, indeed, constitutes a point of fundamental disagreement between Sartre and other phenomenologists, many of whom would be more in agreement with Frederick A. Olafson's claim that the self, like an iceberg, can be exposed only partially and only if other portions are submerged: "this amounts to saying that while none of the multiple relationships we continuously sustain to the whole of our human environment is immune to becoming the object of critical attention and revisionary choice, it is not possible for all such relationships to be subject to such a review simultaneously or continuously without grave consequences for the integrity of the very moral life they compose."[48]

In fact, Sartre seems to call the possibility of such transparency into question, at least as it pertains to human relationships, when he says, in *Search for a Method*: "the opaqueness of direct human relations comes from this fact, that they are always conditioned by others."[49] Although much light can be shed on this multiple conditioning, it is difficult to see how total transparency can be achieved. Whatever Sartre thought of it, total transparency seems best interpreted as one of those impossible ideals which, though not directly sought by the authentic, serve to regulate their actions by always challenging them to effect as much harmony and unity within themselves and with others as is possible.

In *Cahiers*, Sartre sheds a bit more light on this problem of transparency when he discusses how, in aiding another, one not only comprehends the other's end but makes it one's own. Although there is, he says, a preontological comprehension of the original structure of all ends, a preontological comprehension of the other's freedom by my freedom, this is not an intuitive comprehension; rather, "it presupposes an active original intention that is the basis of its revelation. The end of the other is able to appear to me as end only in and by the outlining of the adoption of this end by myself." I engage myself but nonetheless recognize that the end is not mine. To will this end authentically, I must will "that the end be realized by the other." In choosing to aid another, I will that

> the world have an infinity of free and finite futures of which each would be directly projected by a free will and indirectly sustained by all the others, insofar as each wills the concrete freedom of the other, that is to say, wills it not in its abstract form of universality but, on the contrary, in its concrete and limited form. Such is the maxim for my action. To will that a value realize itself not because it is mine, not because it is a value, but because it is a value for someone on earth. . . .

In the other's appeal and in the aid I offer in response, there is "refusal to consider the original conflict of freedoms by the look as something impossible to overcome."[50]

Sartre's example of the "human relation of aid" illuminates both the appeal and the aid. His example is a familiar one: "A runs toward the bus; B, on the platform, extends his hand. . . . In grasping it as an instrument, [A] contributes to realizing his own project." Yet, A becomes instrument for B, since A serves as a means to realizing B's end (in this case, that of himself serving as an instrument). A's hand is grasped and pulled; and A becomes an object that is seen, appraised, and pulled, a passivity. Thus, A "feels himself in question in his own freedom." This does not happen against his freedom, however, since he becomes an instrument precisely in pursuing his own end. He discovers the other's freedom, not as opposed and threatening his freedom; rather, "he discovers it at the

heart of his freedom as a free movement of accompany-
ing [him] toward his ends. . . . [Each] freedom is totally
in the other."[51]

With each freedom totally in the other, there seems
to be the kind of transparency here about which Sartre
writes elsewhere. This differs from relations where individuals have a *common project* in the sense, for example, of having the same enemy. Instead, in the
relation of appeal/aid, the one who assists adopts the
other's end in such a way that it *remains the end of the
other and to be realized by the other.* One who aids
responds to the appeal not because the giver of the aid
happens to share the other's end but, rather, because
the other has this end. There is gratuity in the appeal
as well; this, Sartre says, is properly, in fact, that which
makes morality: "From the beginning I recognize that
my end ought to be conditional for the other as it is for
me. That is to say, it ought always to be possible for the
other to refuse aid if the utilized means of aid alter his
own ends."[52] In appealing to the other, one adheres to
the ends of the other: "I sustain them in their concrete
content by my approbation."[53] This is why the appeal
is a "promise of reciprocity," why one does not demand
aid from those whose ends one cannot approve, from
those whom one would not oneself aid.[54]

In the relation appeal/aid, each discovers and wills
the other's freedom, and each is totally in the other.
That is why Sartre sees in the appeal a sketch of a
world he previously called a utopia ("where each treats
the other as an end, that is to say, takes the enterprise
of the other as end")—"a world where each person will
be able to appeal to all the others." That is why, in
addition, Sartre sees an authentic appeal as necessarily
"conscious of being overcoming of all inequality of
condition toward a human world where all appeals of
one person to another might be always possible."[55]

If what Sartre says about the ideal of total transparency is combined with what he says elsewhere about human relationships, his late analysis of fraternity[56] emerges as a viable ideal, vital, as he says, to a moral system: "Fraternity is what human beings will be in relation to each other when through all our history they will be able to say of themselves that they are all bound to each other in feeling and in action."[57]

8

An Ethical Perspective

Our concrete goal—which is a very up-to-date, contemporary one—is human liberation. It has three aspects. To begin with, the metaphysical liberation of man: making him aware of his total freedom and his duty to struggle against everything which tends to limit his freedom. Second, his artistic freedom: making the free man's communication with other men easier thanks to works of art, and by this means immersing others in an atmosphere of freedom. Third, his political and social liberation: liberating the oppressed.
—"Jean-Paul Sartre in Berlin: Discussion of *The Flies*"

What emerges from a careful study of Sartre's work is an ethical perspective that well deserves a place of prominence among contemporary ethical theories. It is a position that affirms freedom, choice, and ambiguity, that recognizes the problems such concepts present to ethics and offers solutions to these problems.

In this book, I have argued, first, that Sartre presents a notion of authenticity which, at least implicitly, provides solutions to various problems recognized by traditional ethicists. I maintain that Sartre offers a way of affirming universalizability in moral judgments without either adopting a Kantian view of human reason or importing an unsupported and unsupportable "absolute" value (such as consistency) into his ethics.

Second, I have indicated how Sartre's ethics affirms a dialectic closely resembling that of Hegel as a way of avoiding and overcoming a particular kind of alienation. Admittedly, not all alienation can be overcome; some alienation is fundamental to the human condition. Still, there is a kind of alienation—self-alienation—that Sartre recognizes as avoidable.

Third, I have shown that relativism and futility present special problems to Sartrean ethics, problems that are resolved by Sartre's notion of play.

Fourth, I have distinguished, on the level of societies, what Sartre recognizes as a fundamental, non-eliminable alienation from a kind of alienation that is not fundamental and that can be eliminated. On the basis of this distinction, Sartre can criticize oppressive societies as he criticizes individuals who fail to recognize and affirm the freedom of others.

Fifth, I have explored the possibilities of a love that approaches the other with confidence in freedom and with trust and generosity. Although sequestration and individualism play a major role in Sartre's writings, there are nevertheless a number of indications of a kind of love that affirms freedom, that respects the other as an end. Once again, Sartre can affirm an aspect of Kantian ethics—the kingdom of ends—without at the same time affirming the Kantian view of humanity.

With these analyses of problems and resolutions, the possibilities and viability of a Sartrean ethics become clearer. This is not to say that Sartre would have pursued the possibilities of ethics in just these ways. All that can be said is that, given Sartre's published work, the foregoing is the picture of ethics that emerges when the various hints and assertions are brought together and analyzed.

At the end of a book on Sartrean ethics it is fitting to say something about the fact that Sartre never published the work on ethics he promised the readers of *Being and Nothingness*. Sartre's own explanation seems to be that his discovery of more pressing problems, such as starvation, rendered trivial further study of individual bad faith and authenticity: "The universe is still dark. We are disaster-ridden animals. . . . But I discovered abruptly that alienation, man's exploitation by man, and undernourishment relegated metaphysical evil, which is a luxury, to the background. Hunger is an evil, period."[1]

Even so, why did Sartre not publish the book on ethics that was substantially completed? For an answer to this question, we should, I believe, turn to a relatively early work of Sartre's, *Anti-Semite and Jew*, in which he recognized that "metaphysical uneasiness is a condition that the Jew—no more than the worker—cannot allow himself today." This is because, Sartre continues: "One must be sure of one's rights and firmly rooted in the world, one must be free of the fears that each day assail oppressed minorities or classes, before one dare raise questions about the place of man in the world and his eternal destiny."[2]

Given Sartre's growing awareness that substantial portions of humanity stand in need of liberation, by not publishing his ethics perhaps he was merely postponing further "metaphysics" until the time when human beings are liberated or at least until he had published those works he thought would be more instrumental in effecting this liberation.[3] As he says, when human beings are liberated, metaphysics "will again become an essential concern of mankind."[4] In discussing *The Devil and the Good Lord*, de Beauvoir observes, "In 1944, Sartre thought that any situation could be transcended by subjective effort; in 1951, he knew that circumstances can sometimes steal our transcendence from us; in that case, no individual salvation is possible, only a collective struggle."[5]

Sartre's reasoning in his early work on ethics, unpublished in his own lifetime, also led him to the recognition that one cannot make the conversion alone, that "morality isn't possible unless all the world is moral."[6] This recognition, in turn, led him, in *Cahiers*, into a rather sticky problem concerning violence. First, violence is connected in a number of ways with ethics of obligation, of "ought," of "right." On the individual level, such an ethics alienates individuals from themselves. Exigency or obligation can come only from others; thus it is fundamentally alienating to the individual from the outset.[7] The individual is alienated from her or his freedom since "there is freedom only when the choice is choice of an end outside of the means which permit it to be attained." As Sartre said, "My free choice postulates some values and some objects of value. It cannot pose obligations." Consequently, "[the] person who acts from duty *doesn't recognize himself in his work.*"[8]

Beyond this, obligation alienates an individual from his or her end by turning the individual into a means. The end, being absolute, is the essential; the human is the nonessential. This results in the sacrifice of humanity to the end and, if the end is humanity or the city of ends, in the collapse of the end.[9] Making any end absolute, as does the ethics of obligation, can all too easily justify violence, inasmuch as any means is warranted by such an end (the end justifies the means—the maxim of violence).

This alienation becomes even more problematic by

virtue of a practical connection which Sartre saw between right and violence. According to Sartre, right arises only in periods of injustice; it would disappear in a harmonious, egalitarian society. Moreover, this right allegedly prohibits violence, thus serving to legitimate and secure the status quo and the previous violence on which the status quo in question is always based: "Thus, the right is an absolute refusal of the violence which can serve only the oppressor because the violence whence the right has come is anterior to the establishment of right and because the concrete inequality is entirely outside the juridical realm."[10] Sartre illustrated this point with an example of an American Jewish captain refused entry to a public place by the proprietor. The proprietor justifies himself by appealing to the laws of property: it is his establishment, and he has the right to dispose of his property as he sees fit. While the proprietor does violence to the captain, according to Sartre, on the material plane, by treating him in terms of "his corporeal particularity" (his Jewishness) rather than as a "concrete freedom," he puts the captain in an untenable position: "in entering by force, the captain would have made an attempt against the *formal freedom* of the proprietor, that is to say, against his freedom to enjoy that which he possesses."[11]

The oppressed, in general, are in a situation parallel to that of the Jewish captain. For example, for a slave to revolt is objectively a crime: "it is defined as such by the order of the master, it is resented as such by the resigned. Subjectively, it is resented as the Bad, the Crime, the Sacrilege, the systematic destruction of the Human, the Refusal of Time."[12] Although the revolt is free choice and at least not an actualizing of the good of the other, it is "still not *a Good* because the values of the master obstruct the view in order to constitute another Good."[13] Worse, though, revolt is violence and thus, as we have seen, in conflict with the good in the name of which it might operate (the city of ends). Revolt may be necessary; the only recourse freedom has "[when] the Good is alienated . . . in the hands of the Other," "necessarily a progress toward freedom."[14] At the same time, it clearly illustrates that morality is possible only when all the world is moral.

What one says about morality may therefore make the already untenable position of the revolutionary seem all the more so. Oppression stands in the way of morality, the creation of the city of ends; it stands in the way of developing an ethics, too, since the latter can all too easily be co-opted by the system of oppression in support of itself. Sartre tries to affirm the violence of revolt as moral when he presents as a "moral law" the following: "in the case of *impossibility,* the choice of Good leads to a reinforcing of the impossible, it is necessary to choose Evil in order to find Good." This, however, seems to evince Sartre's own struggle with himself, since he already has presented clearly the way in which violence (as part of the organic unity of the means) is "alteration of the total series of means and therefore of the end." That is, it may be necessary; but, it seems, it never can be justified. It must be condemned by the morality of right against which it revolts and by the morality of the city of ends as well, toward which the revolt may indeed be a progress. As Sartre says, "if the goal is concrete and finite, if it is in a future to the measure of a man [*dans un avenir à mesure d'homme*], it ought to exclude violence (if it is not itself to be violence and evil); and if one is obliged to resort to it in order to attain it, at least it appears unjustifiable and *limited.* This will be the failure at the heart of the result."[15] Perhaps this dilemma is what Sartre has in mind when he says, in *Saint Genet:* "*any* ethic is both impossible and necessary."[16]

This helps explain why, instead of publishing his work on ethics, Sartre turned to an analysis of collectives in his *Critique of Dialectical Reason* and to an attempt to clarify the individual existence of Flaubert in *The Idiot of the Family*. In both works he tries to correct deficiencies in Marxism. In the *Critique* he expands the Marxist view of alienation, reintroduces the questioner into the investigation of man[17] and thereby incorporates his earlier "existential" view of freedom into Marxism. In *The Idiot of the Family*, by tracing Flaubert's childhood and his continuing relations with his father, mother, brother, sister, and society, Sartre shows how Flaubert—and, for that matter, any other individual—experiences his alienation and reification: "*first*, as a child, *in his parents' work*," rather than first in his own work as an adult. The latter, he thinks, corrects a deficiency of "today's Marxists" who, forgetting their own childhoods, "are concerned only with adults; reading them, one would believe that we are born at the age when we earn our first wages."[18]

Thus, in his own later writing, Sartre seems to hold in a tension the opposing elements he had stressed in *What Is Literature?*: "the freedom of the person *and* the socialist revolution."[19] In the *Critique*, Sartre delineates the power of collectivities to overcome starvation and oppression. In his study of Flaubert, he demonstrates and refines a method of making one man's existence visible to another, even in a society that tends to mask or hide individuals from each other. The importance of such visibility can be seen in the interview with Sartre, "Self-Portrait at Seventy," where he says: "A man's existence must be entirely visible to his neighbor, whose own existence must be entirely visible in turn, before true social harmony can be established."[20]

Whereas, in *Search for a Method*, Sartre claims "that the opaqueness of direct human relations comes from this fact, that they are always conditioned by others,"[21] he later seemed to reconsider whether human beings must to some extent be opaque to each other. In "Self-Portrait at Seventy," he denies that complete visibility can be realized without "a change in the economic, cultural, and affective relations among men."[22] Nonetheless, in his presentation of Flaubert, he may be attempting to demonstrate a method and to keep before us what is required on an individual level once that revolution is achieved. Of his work on Flaubert, Sartre wrote: "The fundamental project in my 'Flaubert' is to show that at bottom everything can be communicated . . . that every human project is perfectly capable of being understood if the appropriate methods are used and the necessary documents are available."[23]

Notes

1. Is an Ethics of Deliverance and Salvation Possible?

1. Sartre, *Being and Nothingness*, trans. Hazel E. Barnes (New York: Philosophical Library, 1956), p. 581.

2. Ibid., pp. 70n., 412n.

3. Ibid., pp. 615, 627.

4. Thomas C. Anderson, *The Foundation and Structure of Sartrean Ethics* (Lawrence: The Regents Press of Kansas, 1979), p. 149.

5. Herbert Marcuse, "Sartre's Existentialism," in *Studies in Critical Philosophy*, trans. Joris de Bres (Boston: Beacon Press, 1972), p. 174.

6. Ibid., p. 189.

7. Sartre, "Materialism and Revolution," in *Literary and Philosophical Essays*, trans. Annette Michelson (New York: Collier Books, 1962), p. 237.

8. "An Interview with Jean-Paul Sartre," in *The Philosophy of Jean-Paul Sartre*, The Library of Living Philosophers, vol. 16, ed. Paul Arthur Schilpp (LaSalle, Ill.: Open Court, 1981), p. 12.

9. Sartre, *Being and Nothingness*, p. 90.

10. "An Interview with Jean-Paul Sartre," p. 20.

11. Sartre, *No Exit*, in *No Exit and Three Other Plays by Jean-Paul Sartre*, trans. Stuart Gilbert (New York: Vintage Books, 1955), p. 47.

12. Iris Murdoch, *Sartre, Romantic Rationalist* (New Haven, Conn.: Yale University Press, 1953), p. 65.

13. "An Interview with Jean-Paul Sartre," p. 13.
14. Ibid., p. 38.
15. Francis Jeanson, *Sartre and the Problem of Morality*, trans. Robert V. Stone (Bloomington: Indiana University Press, 1980), p. 10.

2. Human Being and Bad Faith

1. Sartre, *Being and Nothingness*, p. 615.
2. Ibid., p. lxvii.
3. Maurice Natanson, *A Critique of Jean-Paul Sartre's Ontology* (Lincoln, Nebr.: University of Nebraska Studies, 1951), pp. 95–96.
4. Sartre, *Being and Nothingness*, pp. 625–26.
5. Ibid., p. li.
6. Ibid., p. 49.
7. Ibid., p. lx.
8. Ibid., pp. lxv, lxvi.
9. Ibid., p. lxvi.
10. Ibid., p. lxvii.
11. Ibid., pp. 82–83.
12. Ibid., p. 58.
13. Ibid.
14. Sartre, *Cahiers pour une morale* (Paris: Gallimard, 1983), p. 101.
15. Maurice Merleau-Ponty, "Sartre and Ultrabolshevism," *Adventures of the Dialectic*, trans. Joseph Bien (Evanston, Ill.: Northwestern University Press, 1973), pp. 147, 98.
16. This is not, of course, to say that Sartre's view did not evolve in important ways over the years. Although it seems clear to me that Sartre's was never a philosophy of "the pure subject," I think Sartre (de Beauvoir, *Adieux*, trans. Patrick O'Brian [New York: Pantheon Books, 1984], p. 358) is correct to characterize his view of freedom as moving from the Stoic view "that one was always free, even in exceedingly dis-

agreeable circumstances that might end in death" to the recognition that "there are situations in which one cannot be free." Sartre dates this change "toward 1942–43 or perhaps even a little later."

17. Sartre, *Cahiers,* p. 74.

18. Sartre, *Being and Nothingness,* p. 49.

19. Ibid., pp. 49–50.

20. Herbert Fingarette, *Self-Deception* (New York: Humanities Press, 1969), p. 63.

21. Ibid.

22. Ibid., p. 53.

23. Sartre, *Being and Nothingness,* p. 50n.

24. Ibid., p. 50.

25. As Sartre notes (ibid.) this "does not mean that he does not have abrupt awakenings to cynicism or to good faith, but . . . implies a constant and particular style of life."

26. Ibid., p. 68.

27. Fingarette, *Self-Deception,* p. 99.

28. Sartre, *Being and Nothingness,* p. 51.

29. Ibid., p. 53.

30. Ibid., pp. 53–55.

31. Ibid., p. 56.

32. Ibid., pp. 59–60.

33. Arthur C. Danto, *Jean-Paul Sartre* (New York: Viking Press, 1975), pp. 77–78.

34. Simone de Beauvoir, *The Ethics of Ambiguity,* trans. Bernard Frechtman (New York: Citadel Press, 1964), pp. 35–38.

35. D. Z. Phillips, "Bad Faith and Sartre's Waiter," *Philosophy* 56, no. 215 (January 1981).

36. Sartre, *Being and Nothingness,* p. 59.

37. Phillips, "Bad Faith and Sartre's Waiter," p. 25.

38. Thomas R. Flynn, *Sartre and Marxist Existentialism: The Test Case of Collective Responsibility* (Chicago: University of Chicago Press, 1984), p. 30.

39. Sartre, "Materialism and Revolution," pp. 198–256.

40. Ibid., p. 245.

41. Sartre, *Being and Nothingness,* p. 56.

42. Ibid., p. 83.
43. Ibid., p. 56.
44. Ibid., p. 81.
45. Jeanson, *Sartre and the Problem of Morality*, p. 14.
46. Robert V. Stone, "Translator's Introduction," Jeanson, *Sartre and the Problem of Morality*, p. xii.
47. M. Merleau-Ponty, *Phenomenology of Perception*, trans. Colin Smith (New York: Humanities Press, 1962), p. 439.
48. Sartre, *Being and Nothingness*, p. 261.
49. Ibid., p. 58.
50. Sartre, *Cahiers*, pp. 230, 240.
51. Sartre, *Being and Nothingness*, p. 58.
52. Sartre (ibid., p. 64) continues: "It is the profound meaning of the saying 'a sin confessed is half pardoned.' The critic demands of the guilty one that he constitute himself as a thing, precisely in order no longer to treat him as a thing."
53. Ibid., p. 65.
54. Ibid., p. 67.
55. Ibid., p. 69.
56. Ibid., p. 68.
57. Ibid., p. 69.
58. Ibid., p. 70.
59. Such hyphenated terms, together with the apparent contradictions presented by Sartre's use of negatives, may seem impossible hurdles to a reader approaching Sartre for the first time. Some of the difficulties surrounding these terms and their usage can be avoided if one always keeps in mind Sartre's definition of man as a being that is what it is not and is not what it is, as well as clarifications of this definition by the three sets of double properties.
60. Sartre, *Being and Nothingness*, pp. 70, 58.
61. Ibid., p. 64.
62. Sartre, *Anti-Semite and Jew*, trans. George J. Becker (New York: Schocken Books, 1965), p. 90.
63. Sartre, *Cahiers*, pp. 495–96.
64. Alisdair MacIntyre, *After Virtue* (Notre Dame, Ind.: University of Notre Dame Press, 1981), p. 205.

3. Lying to Oneself

1. Originally published in 1946, this popularly written tract has been referred to as "an intellectual street brawl" (James F. Sheridan, Jr., *Sartre: The Radical Conversion* [Athens: Ohio University Press, 1969], p. 18). Apparently because of the widespread misinterpretations to which it gave rise, it was largely rejected by Sartre himself. Yet, because it has been subjected to so many interpretations and because of its treatment of moral judgment, it commands a central place in any study of Sartrean ethics.

2. Sartre, "Existentialism is a Humanism," trans. Philip Mairet, in *Existentialism from Dostoevsky to Sartre*, ed. Walter Kaufmann (New York: World Publishing Company, 1963), p. 307.

3. Ibid.

4. Ibid.

5. Michel Contat and Michel Rybalka, *The Writings of Jean-Paul Sartre*, vol. 1, trans. Richard C. McCleary (Evanston, Ill.: Northwestern University Press, 1974), p. 222.

6. Sartre, "Existentialism is a Humanism," p. 295.

7. Immanuel Kant, *The Moral Law: Kant's Groundwork of the Metaphysics of Morals*, trans. H. J. Paton (New York: Barnes & Noble, 1963), p. 88.

8. Murdoch, *Sartre, Romantic Rationalist*, p. 68.

9. Sartre, *Cahiers*, p. 52.

10. Mary Warnock, *The Philosophy of Sartre* (New York: Barnes and Noble, 1967), pp. 129–34.

11. Sartre, "Existentialism is a Humanism," p. 307.

12. Kant, *Moral Law*, pp. 84–85.

13. Hazel E. Barnes, *An Existentialist Ethics* (New York: Vintage Books, 1967), p. 97.

14. Sartre, *What Is Literature?* trans. Bernard Frechtman (New York: Harper & Row, 1965), pp. 40, 22–23, 56–57, 41.

15. Ibid., p. 41.

16. Sartre, *Anti-Semite and Jew*, pp. 151–53.

17. Sartre, *What Is Literature?* pp. 218, 282.

18. Ibid., p. 282.

19. Sartre, *Cahiers*, p. 188.

20. David Hume, *A Treatise of Human Nature*, ed. L. A. Selby-Bigge (Oxford: The Clarendon Press, 1967), pp. 461–62.

21. de Beauvoir, *Ethics of Ambiguity*, p. 24.

22. Sartre, *Cahiers*, p. 223.

23. Kurt Baier, *The Moral Point of View* (Ithaca, N.Y.: Cornell University Press, 1958), p. 195.

24. Sartre, *Cahiers*, p. 244.

25. Ibid., p. 293.

26. Sartre, "Existentialism is a Humanism," p. 202.

27. Sartre, *Cahiers*, p. 148.

28. de Beauvoir, *Adieux*, p. 363.

29. Peter Caws, *Sartre* (Boston: Routledge & Kegan Paul, 1979), p. 122.

30. For more discussion of Sartre's view of the Jew, see Chapter 4.

31. Sartre, *Cahiers*, p. 448.

32. Ibid., pp. 448–49.

33. Caws, *Sartre*, p. 120.

34. Barnes, *An Existentialist Ethics*, p. 109.

35. Anderson, *The Foundation and Structure of Sartrean Ethics*, pp. 149, 79.

36. This qualification is important, given Sartre's recognition in his war diaries "that there exist in me a certain number of full, effective willings which are nonetheless not conjoined with realization" (*The War Diaries of Jean-Paul Sartre*, trans. Quintin Hoare [New York: Pantheon Books, 1984], p. 36). For some of these willings, there simply is, at the moment, nothing to do, given the "faraway" nature of the decision, such as his intention to answer a letter "tomorrow" or his decisions concerning his more distant return to civilian life. Even in the war diaries, though, Sartre (p. 35) rejects what he calls "empty volitions" and regards as an "excellent precaution" the "severe, moralistic decision" that judges the intention by the result. Thus in 1939, Sartre clearly saw that "[will] needs the world and the resistance of things." The dreamer, "victim of . . . [his] omnipotence, . . . [is] bound hand and foot by his absolute power" (p. 37).

37. Sartre, *Cahiers*, p. 24.

38. Sartre, *No Exit*, p. 44.
39. Sartre, *Being and Nothingness*, p. 484.
40. "Sartre Accuses the Intellectuals of Bad Faith," interview with John Gerassi, *New York Times Sunday Magazine* (October 17, 1971), p. 119.
41. Sartre, *Cahiers*, p. 223.
42. John Stuart Mill, *Utilitarianism* (Indianapolis: Bobbs-Merrill, 1957), p. 74.
43. Sartre, *Being and Nothingness*, pp. 615, 627.
44. This topic is discussed extensively in Chapter 4.
45. Wilfred Desan, *The Tragic Finale* (New York: Harper, 1960), p. 126.
46. Sartre, *Being and Nothingness*, pp. 49–50.
47. "Believing always falls short: one is never wholly able to believe what he believes since believing involves knowing that one believes and knowing that one believes destroys one's belief" (Sartre, ibid., p. 69).
48. Sartre, *Cahiers*, p. 21.

4. Alienation and Individual Authenticity

1. In order to use the other in my attempt, it seems minimally necessary that that particular other actually see me and that I be able to recognize myself in this seeing.
2. Sartre, "Intimacy," in *The Wall (Intimacy) and Other Stories* trans. Lloyd Alexander (New York: New Directions, 1948), p. 57.
3. Sartre, "Childhood of a Leader," in ibid., p. 142.
4. Sartre, *Being and Nothingness*, p. 363.
5. Ibid.
6. Immanuel Kant, *Critique of Pure Reason*, trans. Norman Kemp Smith (New York: St. Martin's Press, 1961), p. 446.
7. Louis Dupré, "Dialectical Philosophy Before and After Marx," *The New Scholasticism* 46 (Autumn 1972): 493, notes that alienation is not merely objectification but "an externalization *which it knows to be its own.*"

189

8. Sartre, *Being and Nothingness*, pp. 364–65.

9. Sartre (ibid., p. 372) connects this attempt with language since language *"is* originally being-for-others." On the next page he continues: "Language is therefore not distinct from the recognition of the Other's existence . . . [and although this] primitive language is not necessarily seduction . . . seduction does not presuppose any earlier form of language; it is the complete realization of language."

10. Ibid., p. 377.

11. Ibid., pp. 378–79.

12. Ibid., pp. 379–80.

13. Ibid., pp. 381–82.

14. Ibid., p. 394.

15. Ibid., p. 397.

16. Ibid., p. 399.

17. "The proof of this," Sartre continues (ibid., p. 403), "is the fact that he will later live out his abjuration in remorse and shame. Thus he is entirely responsible for it."

18. Ibid., p. 404.

19. Ibid., p. 405.

20. As Sartre (ibid.) says, "he realizes then not only that he has not recovered his *being-outside* but also that the activity by which he seeks to recover it is itself transcended and fixed in 'sadism' as an *habitus* and a property with its cortège of dead-possibilities and that this transformation takes place through and for the Other whom he wishes to enslave."

21. Sartre, *Cahiers*, p. 212.

22. Sartre, *Being and Nothingness*, p. 407.

23. Ibid., p. 408.

24. Ibid.

25. Ibid., pp. 410–12.

26. As Sartre (ibid., p. 412) says, "he who has once been for-others is contaminated in his being for the rest of his days even if the Other should be entirely suppressed; he will never cease to apprehend his dimension of being-for-others as a permanent possibility of his being. He can never recapture what he has alienated; he has even lost all hope of act-

ing on this alienation and turning it to his own advantage since the destroyed Other has carried the key to this alienation along with him to his grave. What I was for the Other is fixed by the Other's death, and I shall irremediably be it in the past."

27. Ibid., p. 412n.

28. When Sartre denies a dialectic of relations with others, he is using "dialectic" in a sense that is in fact distinctly Hegelian: the sense in which there is a movement beyond, an overcoming of, opposition.

29. Warnock, *The Philosophy of Sartre*, p. 99.

30. Contat and Rybalka, *The Writings of Jean-Paul Sartre*, vol. 1, p. 99.

31. G. W. F. Hegel, *Phenomenology of Mind*, trans. J. B. Baillie (New York: Macmillan, 1961), p. 236.

32. Because this encounter seems to be presented as a male/male scenario, I am leaving the pronouns masculine and bequeathing to other scholars questions about the assumed universality of antagonism between consciousnesses and whether Hegel's master/slave dialectic sheds any light on the subordination of women to men. Linda Alcoff and I have written a paper, "Lordship, Bondage, and the Dialectic of Work in Traditional Male/Female Relationships," *Cogito* 2 no. 3 (September 1984): 79–93, which explores limited aspects of the latter question.

33. The master, at least vis-à-vis the slave, is at an impasse. In *Cahiers*, pp. 467, 470, Sartre objected that the inessentiality of the slave does not constitute for the master quite the dialectical problem that Hegel thought it did. Hegel's analysis presumes that the master is alone with the slave, whereas in fact he is not. In the company of other masters, he is recognized in a way that compensates for the failure of recognition he experiences with his slave.

34. Hegel, *Phenomenology*, p. 237.

35. Ibid., pp. 236–42. See the commentary on Hegel's "Lordship and Bondage" by Alexandre Kojève, *Introduction to the Reading of Hegel*, trans. James H. Nichols, Jr. (New York: Basic Books, 1969), pp. 21–22.

36. Sartre, *Critique of Dialectical Reason*, trans. Alan Sheridan-Smith (Atlantic Highlands, N.J.: Humanities Press, 1976), p. 158.

37. Sartre (*Being and Nothingness*, p. 370) himself notes the parallel between his lover and beloved and Hegel's master and slave, pointing out the difference: "the master demands the slave's freedom only laterally and, so to speak, implicitly, while the lover wants the beloved's freedom *first and foremost.*"

38. Murdoch, *Sartre, Romantic Rationalist*, p. 65.

39. Ibid.

40. Sartre, *Cahiers*, p. 487.

41. Alisdair MacIntyre, "Existentialism," in *Sartre*, ed. Mary Warnock (Garden City, N.Y.: Doubleday, 1971), p. 33.

42. Sartre, *Being and Nothingness*, p. 90.

43. Neither the impasse of the individuals described in *Being and Nothingness* nor the impasse of Hegel's master rules out a dialectic in history. The point is just that neither the master nor the individuals in Sartre's circle of relations seem to be themselves capable of any dialectical overcoming of their respective positions.

44. Sartre, *Being and Nothingness*, p. 412.

45. de Beauvoir, *Ethics of Ambiguity*, p. 13.

46. Norman N. Greene, *Jean-Paul Sartre, The Existentialist Ethic* (Ann Arbor, Mich.: Ann Arbor Paperbacks, 1966), p. 32.

47. R. M. Hare, *The Language of Morals* (Oxford: Clarendon Press, 1952), p. 78.

48. Ibid., p. 69.

49. Sartre, *Cahiers*, p. 22.

50. Sartre, "Merleau-Ponty," in *Situations*, trans. Benita Eisler (Greenwich, Conn.: Fawcett, 1965), p. 161n.; Sartre, *Cahiers*, p. 13.

51. Ibid., p. 42.

52. See Iris Murdoch, "Hegel in Modern Dress," *New Statesman* 53 (May 25, 1957): 676.

53. Sartre, *Saint Genet*, trans. Bernard Frechtman (New York: New American Library, 1964), pp. 35, 166–67, 187, 203.

54. That poetry is a step on the way toward conversion and authenticity is made clear in *Cahiers* (p. 46) where Sartre says: "Poetry saves the failure as such, persuades man that there is an absolute. This absolute is man. But it doesn't say it clearly. Poetry is the salute to the pursuit of Being seen from the point of view of a nonconverted reflection."

55. Sartre, *Saint Genet*, p. 626.

56. de Beauvoir, "Merleau-Ponty et le pseudo-Sartrisme," in *Les Temps Modernes* (Juin–Juillet, 1955): 2079.

57. Sartre, *Saint Genet*, pp. 203, 373–74.

58. Ibid., p. 374.

59. Ibid., p. 433.

60. Ibid., p. 590.

61. Ibid., pp. 612–13.

62. Ibid., p. 613.

63. Ibid., p. 621.

64. Sartre, *Cahiers*, p. 453.

65. Sartre, *Saint Genet*, pp. 617, 621.

66. Sartre, "The Wall," *Existentialism from Dostoevsky to Sartre*, ed. Walter Kaufmann (New York: World Publishing, 1963), p. 239.

67. Sartre, *The Devil and the Good Lord*, trans. Kitty Black in *The Devil and the Good Lord and Two Other Plays* (New York: Vintage Books, 1960), pp. 143, 145.

68. Ibid., p. 145.

69. de Beauvoir, *Force of Circumstance*, vol. 1, trans. Richard Howard (New York: Harper & Row, 1977), p. 243.

70. Contat and Rybalka, *The Writings of Jean-Paul Sartre*, vol. 1, p. 252.

71. Sartre, *Dirty Hands*, trans. Lionel Abel, in *No Exit and Three Other Plays by Jean-Paul Sartre* (New York: Vintage Books, 1955), pp. 223–25, 246.

72. Sartre, *Anti-Semite and Jew*, pp. 78, 79.

73. Ibid., p. 93.

74. Contat and Rybalka, *The Writings of Jean-Paul Sartre*, vol. 1, p. 145.

75. Sartre, *Cahiers*, p. 411.

76. Sartre, *Anti-Semite and Jew*, p. 79.

77. Ibid., pp. 80, 141.

78. Ibid., p. 141.
79. These changes are discussed in Chapter 6.
80. Sartre, *The Words*, trans. Bernard Frechtman (New York: Fawcett World Library, 1966), p. 160.
81. Sartre, "Letter-Forward," in Jeanson, *Sartre and the Problem of Morality*, p. xxxix.

5. Play versus Seriousness

1. Søren Kierkegaard, *Sickness Unto Death*, in *Fear and Trembling and Sickness Unto Death*, trans. Walter Lowrie (Garden City, N.Y.: Doubleday, 1941), p. 203.
2. John Barth, *The End of the Road* (New York: Doubleday, 1972).
3. W. T. Stace, *The Concept of Morals* (New York: Macmillan, 1962), p. 50.
4. Stace's actual challenge (ibid., p. 58) is that one who becomes an ethical relativist will inevitably "slip" to "some lower and easier standard." Because words like *slip* and *lower* seem to beg the question in favor of absolutism, I consider only what remains of Stace's criticism, after the removal of the question-begging elements.
5. Anderson, *Foundation and Structure of Sartrean Ethics*, p. 149.
6. Sartre, *Being and Nothingness*, p. 627.
7. Anderson, *Foundation and Structure of Sartrean Ethics*, pp. 28–31, 56.
8. Sartre, *Saint Genet*, pp. 612–13, 617.
9. Sartre, *Critique of Dialectical Reason*, pp. 668, 678.
10. Ibid., pp. 538–39.
11. Sartre, *Cahiers*, p. 42.
12. Immanuel Kant, *Critique of Practical Reason*, trans. Lewis White Beck (New York: Bobbs-Merrill, 1956), p. 127.
13. William Leon McBride, "Jean-Paul Sartre: Man, Freedom and Praxis," in *Existential Philosophers: Kierkegaard to Merleau-Ponty*, ed. George Alfred Schrader (New York: McGraw-Hill, 1967), p. 286.

14. Douglas Kirsner, *The Schizoid World of Jean-Paul Sartre* (Atlantic Highlands, N.J.: Humanities Press, 1977), p. 22.

15. Ralph Netzky, "Playful Freedom," *Philosophy Today* 18 (Summer 1974): 125–36.

16. Sartre, *Being and Nothingness*, p. 580.

17. Ibid., pp. 580–81.

18. Ibid., p. 581.

19. Sartre, *Cahiers*, p. 388.

20. Ibid., p. 464.

21. Merleau-Ponty, "Sartre and Ultrabolshevism," p. 195.

22. Ibid., p. 196.

23. Sartre, "Materialism and Revolution," p. 237.

24. Jeanson, *Sartre and the Problem of Morality*, p. 179.

25. Ibid., p. 178.

26. Sartre, *Being and Nothingness*, pp. 161, 155.

27. Sartre, *Cahiers*, p. 19.

28. Ibid., p. 494.

29. Ibid., p. 575.

30. Søren Kierkegaard, *Kierkegaard's Concluding Unscientific Postscript*, trans. David F. Swenson (Princeton: Princeton University Press, 1941), p. 421.

31. Søren Kierkegaard, *Either/Or*, vol. 2, trans. Walter Lowrie (Garden City, N.Y.: Doubleday, 1959), p. 352.

32. Kierkegaard, *Kierkegaard's Concluding Unscientific Postscript*, p. 466.

33. Sartre, "Existentialism is a Humanism," p. 292.

34. "The Last Words of Jean-Paul Sartre, An Interview with Benny Levy," trans. Adrienne Foulke, *Dissent* (Fall 1980): 398.

35. de Beauvoir, *Adieux*, p. 111.

36. Barnes, *An Existentialist Ethics*, pp. 94–95, offers a similar interpretation of unity or coincidence as a regulative ideal.

37. Sartre, *Cahiers*, pp. 109–10.

38. Ibid., pp. 175, 180, 182, 183, 211.

39. Ibid., pp. 180, 451, 175, 216.

40. Ibid., p. 463.

41. "The Last Words of Jean-Paul Sartre," p. 399.

42. Sartre, *Cahiers*, p. 406.
43. Ibid., p. 249.
44. "The Last Words of Jean-Paul Sartre," p. 400.
45. Sartre, *Being and Nothingness*, p. 627.
46. Ibid., p. 59.
47. Netzky, "Playful Freedom," p. 135.
48. Sartre, *The Emotions*, trans. Bernard Frechtman (New York: Philosophical Library, 1948), pp. 62–63.
49. Joseph P. Fell, *Heidegger and Sartre* (New York: Columbia University Press, 1979), p. 141.
50. Sartre, *Iron in the Soul*, trans. Gerard Hopkins (Harmondsworth, Middlesex: Penguin Books, 1971), p. 222.
51. Ibid., p. 87.
52. Sartre, *Cahiers*, p. 54.

6. Alienation and Society

1. István Mészáros, *Marx's Theory of Alienation* (New York: Harper & Row, 1972), p. 244.
2. Ibid.
3. Sartre, *Being and Nothingness*, pp. 416–17.
4. Ibid., p. 418.
5. Ibid., pp. 413–14.
6. Ibid., p. 425.
7. Martin Heidegger, *Being and Time*, trans. John Macquarrie and Edward Robinson (New York: Harper & Row, 1962), p. 164.
8. Sartre, *Being and Nothingness*, p. 427.
9. Sartre, *The Devil and the Good Lord*, p. 145.
10. Sartre, *Being and Nothingness*, pp. 424–25.
11. Murdoch, *Sartre, Romantic Rationalist*, p. 65.
12. Merleau-Ponty, "Sartre and Ultrabolshevism," p. 152.
13. Sartre, *Being and Nothingness*, p. 426.
14. Ibid., p. 429.
15. Ibid., p. 290.
16. Ibid., p. 425.
17. Contat and Rybalka, *The Writings of Jean-Paul Sartre*, vol. 1, p. 113.

18. Sartre, *Critique of Dialectical Reason*, pp. 102, 91.

19. Ibid., p. 231.

20. Sartre, "A More Precise Characterization of Existentialism," in Contat and Rybalka, *The Writings of Jean-Paul Sartre*, vol. 2, p. 159.

21. Sartre, *Critique of Dialectical Reason*, p. 232.

22. Sartre, *The Chips Are Down*, trans. Louise Varése (New York: Lear, 1948), p. 80.

23. *Praxis* is defined in the glossary of *Critique of Dialectical Reason*, p. 829, as "the activity of an individual or group in organising conditions in the light of some end."

24. See Sartre, *Anti-Semite and Jew*, originally published as *Reflexions sur la Question Juive* in 1946.

25. Sartre, *Cahiers*, p. 342.

26. Sartre, *Critique of Dialectical Reason*, p. 250.

27. Ibid., pp. 128, 130.

28. Ibid., pp. 331–32.

29. Hubert L. Dreyfus and Piotr Hoffman, "Sartre's Changed Conception of Consciousness: From Lucidity to Opacity," in *The Philosophy of Jean-Paul Sartre*, Library of Living Philosophers, vol. 16, ed. Schilpp (La Salle, Ill.: Open Court, 1981), p. 230.

30. Sartre, "Materialism and Revolution," p. 245.

31. Sartre, *Cahiers*, p. 344.

32. Sartre, Introduction to *Les Temps Modernes*, in *Paths to the Present*, ed. Eugen Weber (New York: Dodd, Mead, 1964), p. 441.

33. Sartre, *Search for a Method*, trans. Hazel E. Barnes (New York: Alfred A. Knopf, 1967), p. 8.

34. William Leon McBride, "Sartre and Marxism," in *The Philosophy of Jean-Paul Sartre*, p. 606.

35. Sartre, *Critique of Dialectical Reason*, pp. 272–73.

36. For further discussion of such alienation, see the treatments of the inevitability of alienation in Richard Schacht, *Alienation* (Garden City, N.Y.: Doubleday, 1970), pp. xv–lviii, 234–39, and in Walter Kaufmann, *Without Guilt and Justice* (New York: Peter H. Wyden, 1973), p. 140.

37. Sartre, *Critique of Dialectical Reason*, p. 274.

38. Ibid., p. 227.

39. Ibid., p. 228.

40. Sartre, *Iron in the Soul*, p. 217.
41. Ibid., p. 225.
42. Sartre, *Critique of Dialectical Reason*, p. 227.
43. Sartre, *Cahiers*, p. 87.
44. Sartre, *Critique of Dialectical Reason*, pp. 136, 112.
45. Ibid., pp. 208, 206.
46. Ibid., p. 208.
47. Sartre, *Cahiers*, p. 345.
48. Ibid., pp. 403–404.
49. Ibid., p. 404.
50. Sartre, *Critique of Dialectical Reason*, pp. 316, 351–63.
51. Ibid., p. 316.
52. Ibid., pp. 178, 536–37.
53. Thomas R. Flynn, "Mediated Reciprocity and the Genius of the Third," in *The Philosophy of Jean-Paul Sartre*, pp. 354–56. For a more complete analysis of the way the Third operates in the formation of the Group, see the rest of Flynn's essay.
54. Sartre, *Critique of Dialectical Reason*, p. 540.
55. F. H. Bradley, "Essay V: My Station and its Duties," *Ethical Studies* (London: Oxford University Press, 1962), pp. 202–06.
56. Sartre, *Critique of Dialectical Reason*, pp. 538–39.
57. Flynn, *Sartre and Marxist Existentialism*, p. 201.
58. Sartre, *Critique of Dialectical Reason*, p. 425.
59. Ibid., p. 433.
60. Ibid., pp. 609, 636.
61. Ibid., p. 678.
62. Ibid., p. 668.
63. See Warnock, *The Philosophy of Sartre*, p. 135.
64. Pietro Chiodi, *Sartre and Marxism*, trans. Kate Soper (Atlantic Highlands, N.J.: Humanities Press, 1976), p. 100.
65. Sartre, *Critique of Dialectical Reason*, p. 227.
66. Chiodi, *Sartre and Marxism*, p. x.
67. Contat and Rybalka, *The Writings of Jean-Paul Sartre*, vol. 1, p. 222.
68. Sartre, *Cahiers*, pp. 365, 371.
69. Sartre, *No Exit*, p. 44.
70. But it is important to note the contrast between the

purposeful, earnest activity of such societies and the play of Sartre and his playmates, as this is described in *The Words* (p. 139): "Our games 'overexcited' us, as our mothers said, and at times transformed our group into a unanimous little crowd that swallowed me up. But we could never forget our parents for long; their invisible presence made us quickly relapse into the shared solitude of animal groups. Aimless, purposeless, without a hierarchy, our society wavered between total fusion and juxtaposition."

71. I find it interesting that Flynn also writes of "intimations," though in a different context. He suggests (*Sartre and Marxist Existentialism*, p. 204) that Sartre died "with intimations of his goal": "Such is Sartre, the lonely thinker, apostle of individual responsibility, for whom the Other's existence was man's original fall, gradually discovering in the contingencies of history the need and the joy of communal action. It is as if the small boy who so wanted an invitation to play with the others in the Luxembourg Gardens had finally, at mid-life, been allowed to join in and, in his old age, had come to champion this hard-won sense of brotherhood as the model and goal of what it is to be human. 'A whole man, composed of all men and as good as all of them and no better than any,' but in the company of men."

72. Sartre, "A More Precise Characterization of Existentialism," in Contat and Rybalka, *The Writings of Jean-Paul Sartre*, vol. 2, p. 159.

73. Sartre, *What Is Literature?* p. 269.

74. Flynn, *Sartre and Marxist Existentialism*, p. 207.

75. Sartre, *Cahiers*, p. 138.

76. Sartre, *Saint Genet*, p. 626.

7. Sequestration and Love

1. Sartre, *Being and Nothingness*, p. 627.

2. Sartre, *The Words*, pp. 38, 133, 132.

3. Ibid., p. 158.

4. Contat and Rybalka, *The Writings of Jean-Paul Sartre*, vol. 1, pp. 256, 257.

5. de Beauvoir, *Force of Circumstances*, vol. 1, p. 243.

6. Sartre, *What Is Literature?* pp. 17, 18.

7. Sartre, *The Words*, p. 159.

8. Sartre, "The Room," pp. 35, 31.

9. Sartre, *The Condemned of Altona*, trans. Sylvia and George Leeson (New York: Vintage Books, 1961), p. 62.

10. Joseph H. McMahon, *Humans Being: The World of Jean-Paul Sartre* (Chicago: University of Chicago Press, 1971), pp. 112–13n, observes in this play "the use of family relationships as a protection against others."

11. Sartre, *Dirty Hands*, pp. 178, 237, 160–61.

12. Sartre, "The Wall," pp. 238–39.

13. Sartre, *Men Without Shadows*, trans. Kitty Black (London: Hamish Hamilton, 1949), pp. 119, 145, 146.

14. Warnock, *The Philosophy of Sartre*, p. 131.

15. Sartre, *The Chips Are Down*, p. 92.

16. Ibid., p. 186.

17. Contat and Rybalka, *The Writings of Jean-Paul Sartre*, vol. 1, pp. 163–64.

18. Sartre, *The Devil and the Good Lord*, pp. 97, 111, 128.

19. Ibid., p. 133. Emphasis added.

20. Ibid., p. 147.

21. McMahon, *Humans Being*, p. 187. Unlike McMahon, I see Hilda as *part* of a "significant development" in Sartre's theory of love and am somewhat wary of his claim that "she represents a kind of feminine force" heralding this "significant development." I fear that seeing her as a "feminine force" may lead McMahon in an unprofitable direction. Anna's love is "feminine" in the sense that she offers Kean a love that is sexual, one that she envisions as involving marriage. Otherwise her love has much in common with that of Hoederer, as the following analysis makes clear. The dangers of importing objectionable societal notions of the feminine into analysis of Sartre's work are adequately shown by Margery L. Collins's and Christine Pierce's analysis of William Barrett's presentation of Sartre ("Holes and Slime: Sexism in Sartre's Psychoanalysis," in *Women and Philosophy*, ed. Carol C. Gould and Marx W. Wartofsky [New York: G. P. Putnam's Sons, 1980], pp. 113–16). At the same time, I should

add that Collins's and Pierce's disparagement of female characters in Sartre's literary works is challenged seriously by characters like Hilda and Anna.

22. Sartre, *Kean*, trans. Kitty Black, *The Devil and the Good Lord and Two Other Plays* (New York: Vintage Books, 1960), pp. 194, 195.

23. Ibid., pp. 213, 220, 276.

24. Sartre, *Cahiers*, p. 26.

25. Sartre, *Critique of Dialectical Reason*, p. 439; Sartre, *The Devil and the Good Lord*, p. 145.

26. See McMahon's discussion in *Humans Being*, p. 117.

27. Contat and Rybalka, *The Writings of Jean-Paul Sartre*, vol. 1, p. 254.

28. Sartre, *Dirty Hands*, p. 233.

29. Sartre, *What Is Literature?* p. 269.

30. Sartre, *The Devil and the Good Lord*, p. 145.

31. Ibid., pp. 111, 146.

32. Sartre, *Kean*, p. 279.

33. Ibid., p. 256.

34. Sartre, *Cahiers*, pp. 430, 523.

35. Sartre, *Being and Nothingness*, p. 371.

36. Sartre, *What Is Literature?* p. 52.

37. Ibid., p. 53.

38. Ibid., p. 49.

39. Sartre, *Being and Nothingness*, p. 409.

40. Sartre, *Cahiers*, p. 95.

41. Ibid., pp. 202, 201, 203.

42. Ibid., p. 216.

43. Sartre, *Being and Nothingness*, p. 408.

44. Sartre, "Merleau-Ponty," p. 205.

45. Ibid., p. 221.

46. Sartre, "Self-Portrait at Seventy," in *Life/Situations*, trans. Paul Auster and Lydia Davis (New York: Pantheon, 1977), p. 12.

47. Ibid., p. 13.

48. Frederick A. Olafson, *Principles and Persons* (Baltimore: Johns Hopkins University Press, 1967), p. 250.

49. Sartre, *Search for a Method*, p. 80.

50. Sartre, *Cahiers*, pp. 288, 290, 292, 293.

51. Ibid., p. 299.

52. Ibid., pp. 296, 295.

53. Ibid., p. 296.

54. Ibid., pp. 295–96.

55. Ibid., pp. 54, 296–97.

56. de Beauvoir, *Adieux*, p. 119, expresses her outrage over statements Levy "extorted" from Sartre, including the weakening of the notion of fraternity, a notion which, she says, had been "so strong and firm in the *Critique of Dialectical Reason.*" Levy does try to get Sartre to agree that talk of fraternity is "mythology."

57. "The Last Words of Jean-Paul Sartre," p. 414.

8. An Ethical Perspective

1. Contat and Rybalka, *The Writings of Jean-Paul Sartre*, vol. 1, p. 447.

2. Sartre, *Anti-Semite and Jew*, p. 133.

3. Contat and Rybalka, *The Writings of Jean-Paul Sartre*, vol. 1, p. 449, report that Sartre continued to write about ethics in 1964–65 and at the beginning of 1969 and told them that "his dialectical ethics was entirely composed in his mind and that the only remaining problems he foresaw were problems of writing it up."

4. Sartre, *Anti-Semite and Jew*, p. 133.

5. Contat and Rybalka, *The Writings of Jean-Paul Sartre*, vol. 1, p. 249.

6. Sartre, *Cahiers*, p. 16.

7. Ibid., p. 147.

8. Ibid., pp. 265, 256, 267.

9. Ibid., pp. 212, 216.

10. Ibid., p. 150.

11. Ibid., p. 151.

12. Ibid., p. 416.

13. Ibid.

14. Ibid., pp. 418, 419.

15. Ibid., pp. 420, 180, 215–16.

16. Sartre, *Saint Genet*, p. 247.
17. Sartre, *Search for a Method*, p. 175.
18. Ibid., p. 62.
19. Sartre, *What Is Literature?* p. 270.
20. Sartre, "Self-Portrait at Seventy," p. 13.
21. Sartre, *Search for a Method*, p. 80.
22. Sartre, "Self-Portrait at Seventy," p. 13.
23. Contat and Rybalka, *The Writings of Jean-Paul Sartre*, vol. 1, p. 572.

Selected Bibliography

Works by and Interviews with Sartre

This bibliography lists writings by and interviews with Jean-Paul Sartre, in English translation where they exist. The list, while not exhaustive, does include those I have cited or mentioned, as well as others I think bear significantly on ethical issues. They are arranged by the year published in French, or if an interview, by the year during which it was conducted.

1937

"The Wall." In *Existentialism from Dostoevsky to Sartre*, edited by Walter Kaufmann, pp. 223–40. New York: World Publishing Company, 1963.

1938

"Intimacy." Translated by Lloyd Alexander. In *The Wall (Intimacy) and Other Stories*, pp. 55–83. New York: New Directions, 1948.

Nausea. Translated by Lloyd Alexander. Norfolk, Conn.: New Directions Books, 1959.

"The Room." Translated by Lloyd Alexander. In *The Wall*

(Intimacy) and Other Stories, pp. 18–40. New York: New Directions, 1948.

1939

"Childhood of a Leader." Translated by Lloyd Alexander. In *The Wall (Intimacy) and Other Stories*, pp. 84–144. New York: New Directions, 1948.
The Emotions: Outline of a Theory. Translated by Bernard Frechtman. New York: Philosophical Library, 1948.

1943

Being and Nothingness. Translated by Hazel E. Barnes. New York: Philosophical Library, 1956.

1944

"A More Precise Characterization of Existentialism." In *The Writings of Jean-Paul Sartre*, vol. 2, edited by Michel Contat and Michel Rybalka, translated by Richard C. Mc-Cleary, pp. 155–60. Evanston: Northwestern University Press, 1974.
"Paris Alive: The Republic of Silence." Translated by Lincoln Kirstein. *Atlantic Monthly* 174 (December 1944): 39–40.

1945

The Age of Reason. Translated by Eric Sutton. *Roads to Freedom*, vol. 1. New York: Bantam Books, 1968.
Introduction to *Les Temps Modernes.* Translated by Françoise Ehrmann. In *Paths to the Present*, edited by Eugene Weber, pp. 432–41. New York: Dodd, Mead, 1964.

No Exit. Translated by Stuart Gilbert. In *No Exit and Three Other Plays by Jean-Paul Sartre,* pp. 1–47. New York: Vintage Books, 1955.
The Reprieve. Translated by Eric Sutton. *Roads to Freedom,* vol. 2. New York: Bantam Books, 1968.

1946

Anti-Semite and Jew. Translated by George J. Becker. New York: Schocken Books, 1965.
"Existentialism is a Humanism." Translated by Philip Mairet. In *Existentialism from Dostoevsky to Sartre,* edited by Walter Kaufmann, pp. 287–311. New York: World Publishing Company, 1963.
"Materialism and Revolution." In *Literary and Philosophical Essays,* translated by Annette Michelson, pp. 198–256. New York: Collier Books, 1962.

1947

The Chips Are Down. Translated by Louise Varése. New York: Lear, 1948.
"Letter-Forward." In Francis Jeanson, *Sartre and the Problem of Morality,* translated and with an introduction by Robert V. Stone, xxxix–xl. Bloomington: Indiana University Press, 1980.
Men without Shadows. Translated by Kitty Black. London: Hamish Hamilton, 1949.

1948

Dirty Hands. Translated by Lionel Abel. In *No Exit and Three Other Plays by Jean-Paul Sartre,* pp. 129–248. New York: Vintage Books, 1955.
In the Mesh. Translated by Mervyn Savill. London: Andrew Dakers, 1954.

"Jean-Paul Sartre in Berlin: Discussion of *The Flies.*" In *The Writings of Jean-Paul Sartre*, vol. 1, edited by Michel Contat and Michel Rybalka, translated by Richard C. McCleary, pp. 199–200. Evanston: Northwestern University Press, 1974.

What Is Literature? Translated by Bernard Frechtman. New York: Harper & Row, 1965.

1949

Iron in the Soul. Translated by Gerard Hopkins. *Roads to Freedom*, vol. 3. Harmondsworth, Middlesex: Penguin Books, 1971.

1951

The Devil and the Good Lord. Translated by Kitty Black. In *The Devil and the Good Lord and Two Other Plays*, pp. 1–149. New York: Vintage Books, 1960.

1952

Saint Genet. Translated by Bernard Frechtman. New York: New American Library, 1964.

1954

"Julius Fucik." In *The Writings of Jean-Paul Sartre*, vol. 2, edited by Michel Contat and Michel Rybalka, translated by Richard C. McCleary, pp. 212–16. Evanston: Northwestern University Press, 1974.

Kean. Translated by Kitty Black. In *The Devil and the Good Lord and Two Other Plays*, pp. 151–279. New York: Vintage Books, 1960.

1957

Search for a Method. Translated by Hazel E. Barnes. New York: Knopf, 1967.

1960

The Condemned of Altona. Translated by Sylvia and George Leeson. New York: Vintage Books, 1961.
Critique of Dialectical Reason. Translated by Alan Sheridan-Smith. Atlantic Highlands, N.J.: Humanities Press, 1976.

1961

"Preface." In Frantz Fanon, *The Wretched of the Earth,* translated by Constance Farrington, pp. 7–26. New York: Grove Press, 1966.

1964

"Merleau-Ponty." In *Situations,* translated by Benita Eisler, pp. 156–226. Greenwich, Conn.: Fawcett, 1965.
The Words. Translated by Bernard Frechtman. New York: Fawcett World Library, 1966.

1967

"Jean-Paul Sartre." *Playboy Interviews,* pp. 162–79. Chicago: Playboy Press, 1967.

1971

The Family Idiot: Gustave Flaubert, 1821–1857. Translated by Carol Cosman. Chicago: University of Chicago Press, 1981.

"Sartre Accuses the Intellectuals of Bad Faith." Interview with John Gerassi. *New York Times Sunday Magazine* (October 17, 1971): 38, 116, 118–19.

1972

Between Existentialism and Marxism. Translated by John Mathews. New York: Pantheon, 1974.

1975

"Conversation with Jean-Paul Sartre." *Oui* (June 1975): 69–70, 122–24, 126.

"An Interview with Sartre." In *The Philosophy of Jean-Paul Sartre.* Library of Living Philosophers, vol. 16, edited by Paul Arthur Schilpp, pp. 5–51. LaSalle, Ill.: Open Court, 1981.

"Simone de Beauvoir Interviews Sartre." In *Life/Situations,* translated by Paul Auster and Lydia Davis, pp. 93–108. New York: Pantheon, 1977.

1976

"An Interview with Jean-Paul Sartre." In *Jean-Paul Sartre: Contemporary Approaches to His Philosophy,* edited by Hugh J. Silverman and Frederick A. Elliston, pp. 221–39. Pittsburgh: Duquesne University Press, 1980.

"Self-Portrait at Seventy." In *Life/Situations,* translated by Paul Auster and Lydia Davis, pp. 3–92. New York: Pantheon, 1977.

1977

"A Conversation about Sex and Women with Jean-Paul Sartre." Interview by Catherine Chaine. *Playboy* (December 1977): 103–104, 116–18, 124, 239.
Sartre by Himself. Translated by Richard Seaver. New York: Urizen Books, 1978.

1980

"The Last Words of Jean-Paul Sartre, An Interview with Benny Levy." Translated by Adrienne Foulke. *Dissent* (Fall 1980): 397–422.

1983

Cahiers pour une morale. Paris: Gallimard, 1983.
The War Diaries. Translated by Quintin Hoare. New York: Pantheon, 1984.

Other Works

Anderson, Thomas C. *The Foundation and Structure of Sartrean Ethics.* Lawrence: The Regents Press of Kansas, 1979.
_____. "Is a Sartrean Ethics Possible?" *Philosophy Today* 14, no. 2/4 (Summer 1970): 116–40.
Aronson, Ronald. *Sartre: Philosophy in the World.* London: Verso, 1980.
_____. *Sartre's Second Critique.* Chicago: University of Chicago Press, 1987.
Arras, John D. "A Critique of Sartrean Authenticity." *The Personalist* 57 (Spring 1976): 171–80.
Baier, Kurt. *The Moral Point of View.* Ithaca, N.Y.: Cornell University Press, 1958.

Barnes, Hazel E. *An Existentialist Ethics.* New York: Vintage Books, 1967.

―――. *Sartre.* New York: Lippincott, 1973.

―――. *Sartre and Flaubert.* Chicago: University of Chicago Press, 1981.

Barrett, William. *Irrational Man.* Garden City, N.Y.: Doubleday, 1962.

Barth, John. *The End of the Road.* New York: Doubleday, 1972.

Bell, Linda A. "Boredom and the Yawn." *Review of Existential Psychology and Psychiatry* 17, no. 1 (1980–81): 91–100.

―――. "Loser Wins: The Importance of Play in a Sartrean Ethics of Authenticity." In *Phenomenology in a Pluralistic Context,* edited by William L. McBride and Calvin O. Schrag, pp. 5–13. Albany: State University of New York Press, 1983.

―――. Review of Thomas C. Anderson, *The Foundation and Structure of Sartrean Ethics. Man and World* 14, no. 2 (1981): 223–27.

―――. "Sartre: Alienation and Society." *Philosophy and Social Criticism* 6, no. 4 (Winter 1979): 409–22.

―――. "Sartre, Dialectic, and the Problem of Overcoming Bad Faith." *Man and World* 10, no. 3 (1973): 292–302.

Bradley, F. H. *Ethical Studies.* London: Oxford University Press, 1962.

Bruening, Sheila M. "Authenticity, Love, and the Reality of Hell: An Existentialist Ethic." *Dialogue* 19, nos. 2–3 (April 1977): 40–51.

Busch, Thomas W. "Coming to Terms with Jean-Paul Sartre: A Critical Review of Recent Books about Sartre." *Philosophy Today* 24, no. 3/4 (Fall 1980): 187–237.

―――. "Sartre: The Phenomenological Reduction and Human Relationships." *Journal of the British Society for Phenomenology* 6, no. 1 (January 1975): 55–61.

Catalano, Joseph S. "Good and Bad Faith." *Review of Existential Psychology and Psychiatry* 17, no. 1 (1980–81): 79–90.

Caws, Peter. *Sartre.* Boston: Routledge & Kegan Paul, 1979.

211

Chiodi, Pietro. *Sartre and Marxism.* Translated by Kate Soper. Atlantic Highlands, N.J.: Humanities Press, 1976.

Collins, Margery, and Christine Pierce. "Holes and Slime: Sexism in Sartre's Psychoanalysis." In *Women and Philosophy,* edited by Carol C. Gould and Marx W. Wartofsky, pp. 112–27. New York: Putnam's, 1980.

Danto, Arthur C. *Jean-Paul Sartre.* New York: Viking, 1975.

de Beauvoir, Simone. *Adieux.* Translated by Patrick O'Brian. New York: Pantheon, 1984.

——. *The Ethics of Ambiguity.* Translated by Bernard Frechtman. New York: Citadel, 1964.

——. *Force of Circumstance.* Translated by Richard Howard. New York: Harper & Row, 1977.

——. "Merleau-Ponty et le pseudo-Sartrisme." *Les Temps Modernes* (Juin–Juillet, 1955): 2072–2122.

Desan, Wilfred. *The Marxism of Jean-Paul Sartre.* Garden City, N.Y.: Doubleday, 1966.

——. *The Tragic Finale.* New York: Harper, 1960.

Dreyfus, Hubert L., and Piotr Hoffman. "Sartre's Changed Conception of Consciousness: From Lucidity to Opacity." In *The Philosophy of Jean-Paul Sartre,* pp. 229–45. See Sartre, "An Interview with Sartre."

Dupré, Louis. "Dialectical Philosophy Before and After Marx." *New Scholasticism* 46 (Autumn 1972): 488–511.

Fell, Joseph P. *Heidegger and Sartre.* New York: Columbia University Press, 1979.

——. "Sartre's Theory of Motivation: Some Clarifications." *Journal of the British Society for Phenomenology* 1, no. 2 (May 1970): 27–34.

Fingarette, Herbert. *Self-Deception.* New York: Humanities Press, 1969.

Flynn, Thomas R. "Mediated Reciprocity and the Genius of the Third." In *The Philosophy of Jean-Paul Sartre,* pp. 345–70. See Sartre, "An Interview with Sartre."

——. *Sartre and Marxist Existentialism: The Test Case of Collective Responsibility.* Chicago: University of Chicago Press, 1984.

Foulk, Gary J. "Plantinga's Criticisms of Sartre's Ethics." *Ethics* 82, no. 4 (July 1972): 330–33.

Frondizi, Risieri. "Sartre's Early Ethics: A Critique." *The Philosophy of Jean-Paul Sartre*, pp. 371–91. See Sartre, "An Interview with Sartre."

Greene, Norman N. *Jean-Paul Sartre, The Existentialist Ethic*. Ann Arbor, Mich.: Ann Arbor Paperbacks, 1966.

Grene, Marjorie. *Introduction to Existentialism*. Chicago: University of Chicago Press, 1948.

————. *Sartre*. New York: New Viewpoints, 1973.

Hare, R. M. *The Language of Morals*. Oxford: Clarendon Press, 1952.

Hartmann, Klaus. *Sartre's Ontology*. Evanston, Ill.: Northwestern University Press, 1966.

Hayim, Gila J. *The Existential Sociology of Jean-Paul Sartre*. Amherst: University of Massachusetts Press, 1980.

Hegel, G. W. F. *Phenomenology of Mind*. Translated by J. B. Baillie. New York: Macmillan, 1961.

Heidegger, Martin. *Being and Time*. Translated by John Macquarrie and Edward Robinson. New York: Harper & Row, 1962.

Hume, David. *A Treatise of Human Nature*. Edited by L. A. Selby-Bigge. Oxford: Clarendon Press, 1967.

Jeanson, Francis. *Sartre and the Problem of Morality*. Translated and with an introduction by Robert V. Stone. Bloomington: Indiana University Press, 1980.

Kant, Immanuel. *Critique of Practical Reason*. Translated by Lewis White Beck. New York: Bobbs-Merrill, 1956.

————. *Critique of Pure Reason*. Translated by Norman Kemp Smith. New York: St. Martin's Press, 1961.

————. *The Moral Law: Kant's Groundwork of the Metaphysics of Morals*. Translated by H. J. Paton. New York: Barnes & Noble, 1963.

Kaufmann, Walter. *Without Guilt and Justice*. New York, Peter H. Wyden, 1973.

Kierkegaard, Søren. *Either/Or*. Translated by Walter Lowrie. Garden City, N.Y.: Doubleday, 1959.

————. *Fear and Trembling and Sickness unto Death*. Translated by Walter Lowrie. Garden City, N.Y.: Doubleday, 1972.

————. *Kierkegaard's Concluding Unscientific Postscript*.

Translated by David F. Swenson. Princeton: Princeton University Press, 1941.

Kirsner, Douglas. *The Schizoid World of Jean-Paul Sartre.* Atlantic Highlands, N.J.: Humanities Press, 1977.

Kojève, Alexandre. *Introduction to the Reading of Hegel.* Translated by James H. Nichols, Jr. New York: Basic Books, 1969.

Kwant, Remy C. "Merleau-Ponty's Criticism of Sartre's Dialectic Philosophy." In *From Phenomenology to Metaphysics,* pp. 130–56. Pittsburgh: Duquesne University Press, 1966.

LaCapra, Dominick, *A Preface to Sartre.* Ithaca, N.Y.: Cornell University Press, 1978.

McBride, William Leon. "Jean-Paul Sartre: Man, Freedom and Praxis." In *Existential Philosophers: Kierkegaard to Merleau-Ponty,* edited by George Alfred Schrader, pp. 261–329. New York: McGraw-Hill, 1967.

————. "Sartre and Marxism." In *The Philosophy of Jean-Paul Sartre,* pp. 605–30. See Sartre, "An Interview with Sartre."

MacIntyre, Alisdair. *After Virtue.* Notre Dame, Ind.: University of Notre Dame Press, 1981.

————. "Existentialism." In *Sartre,* edited by Mary Warnock, pp. 1–58. Garden City, N.Y.: Doubleday, 1971.

McMahon, Joseph H. *Humans Being: The World of Jean-Paul Sartre.* Chicago: University of Chicago Press, 1971.

Marcuse, Herbert. "Sartre's Existentialism." In *Studies in Critical Philosophy,* translated by Joris de Bres, pp. 157–90. Boston: Beacon Press, 1972.

Merleau-Ponty, Maurice. *Phenomenology of Perception.* Translated by Colin Smith. New York: Humanities Press, 1962.

————. "Sartre and Ultrabolshevism." In *Adventures of the Dialectic,* translated by Joseph Bien, pp. 95–201. Evanston: Northwestern University Press, 1973.

Mészáros, István. *Marx's Theory of Alienation.* New York: Harper & Row, 1972.

————. *Search for Freedom, The Work of Sartre,* vol. 1. Atlantic Highlands, N.J.: Humanities Press, 1979.

Mill, John Stuart. *Utilitarianism*. Indianapolis: Bobbs-Merrill, 1957.

Morris, Phyllis Sutton. *Sartre's Concept of a Person*. Amherst: University of Massachusetts Press, 1976.

Murdoch, Iris. "Hegel in Modern Dress." *New Statesman* 53 (May 25, 1975): 675–76.

————. *Sartre, Romantic Rationalist*. New Haven, Conn.: Yale University Press, 1953.

Murphy, Julien S. "The Look in Sartre and Rich." *Hypatia* 2, no. 3 (Summer 1987): 113–24.

Natanson, Maurice. *A Critique of Jean-Paul Sartre's Ontology*. Lincoln: University of Nebraska Studies, 1951.

Netzky, Ralph. "Playful Freedom." *Philosophy Today* 18 (Summer 1974): 125–36.

Olafson, Frederick A. *Principles and Persons*. Baltimore: Johns Hopkins University Press, 1967.

Phillips, D. Z. "Bad Faith and Sartre's Waiter." *Philosophy* 56, no. 215 (January 1981): 23–31.

Plantinga, Alvin. "An Existentialist's Ethics." In *Ethics*, edited by Julius R. Weinberg and Keith E. Yandell. *Problems in Philosophical Inquiry*, vol. 3, pp. 14–27. New York: Holt, Rinehart & Winston, 1971.

Robbins, C. W. "Sartre and the Moral Life." *Philosophy* 52 (October 1977): 409–24.

Santoni, Ronald E. "Sartre on 'Sincerity': 'Bad Faith'? or Equivocation?" *The Personalist* 53 (Spring 1972): 150–60.

Schacht, Richard. *Alienation*. Garden City, N.Y.: Doubleday, 1970.

Schutz, Alfred. "Sartre's Theory of the Alter Ego." In *Collected Papers*, vol. 1, pp. 180–203. The Hague: Martinus Nijhoff, 1964.

Shapiro, Gary. "Choice and Universality in Sartre's Ethics." *Man and World* 7, no. 1 (February 1974): 20–36.

Sheridan, James F., Jr. *Sartre: The Radical Conversion*. Athens: Ohio University Press, 1969.

Smoot, William. "The Concept of Authenticity in Sartre." *Man and World* 7, no. 2 (May 1974): 135–48.

Stace, W. T. *The Concept of Morals*. New York: Macmillan, 1962.

Stern, Alfred. *Sartre.* New York: Dell, 1967.

Stone, Robert V. "Sartre on Bad Faith and Authenticity." In *The Philosophy of Jean-Paul Sartre,* pp. 246–56. See Sartre, "An Interview with Sartre."

Thody, Philip. *Sartre: A Biographical Introduction.* New York: Scribner's, 1971.

Walker, A. D. M. "Sartre, Santoni and Sincerity." *The Personalist* 58 (January 1977): 88–92.

Warnock, Mary. *The Philosophy of Sartre.* New York: Barnes & Noble, 1967.

Index

217

About the Author

Linda A. Bell is Professor of Philosophy, Georgia State University. She received her M.A. from Northwestern University and her B.A. and Ph.D. from Emory University.